the seer

the seer

❖

Jake H. Friesen

Printed in Victoria, Canada

Editing, book design, cover design, and front cover photograph by Steven Lacoursiere
Back cover photograph by Jake Friesen

NATIONAL LIBRARY OF CANADA CATALOGUING IN PUBLICATION DATA

Friesen, Jake
The seer / Jake H. Friesen.
Includes bibliographical references.
ISBN 1-55395-554-4
1. Bible--Prophecies--End of the world.
2. End of the world--Biblical teaching. I. Title.
BT877.F75 2003   236'.9   C2003-900234-9

TRAFFORD

This book was published *on-demand* in cooperation with Trafford Publishing.
On-demand publishing is a unique process and service of making a book available for retail sale to the public taking advantage of on-demand manufacturing and Internet marketing. **On-demand publishing** includes promotions, retail sales, manufacturing, order fulfilment, accounting and collecting royalties on behalf of the author.

Suite 6E, 2333 Government St., Victoria, B.C. V8T 4P4, CANADA
Phone   250-383-686   Toll-free   1-888-232-4444   (Canada   &   US)
Fax   250-383-680   E-mail   sales@trafford.com

Web site www.trafford.com TRAFFORD PUBLISHING IS A DIVISION OF TRAFFORD HOLDINGS LTD.
Trafford Catalogue #02-1270   www.trafford.com/robots/02-1270.html

10   9   8   7   6   5   4   3

Dedication

To Leona, my life's partner, who has encouraged me in writing, and through her sense of realism, has helped me to retain balance and sobriety in this prophetic study.

Acknowledgements

I wish to acknowledge Youth Pastor Blayne Greiner's kind comments in writing the preface for this book.

I thank my grandson, Steven Lacoursiere, for his generous assistance in formatting, and processing the publication.

My thanks also to my daughter Grace Lacoursiere Wulff, for her suggestions on cover designs, formatting, and publishing.

Last, but not least, I acknowledge the host of men and women who through the years of my ministry have given me advice, exhortation, and encouragement in pursuing the divine mandate for God's people for the end times.

Table of Contents

Preface

I have known Jake Friesen for over 20 years and I have seen incredible fruit come from God's prophetic voice speaking through him. He walks in strong godly humility and total accountability to the church.

The church today is in need of the prophetic voice more than any other time in history. Jake is being used by the Lord to encourage and nurture the ministries of pastor, teacher, social work, and counselor, and is actively being used to encourage younger men and women in ministry.

Today is the most exciting time in all of church history, and at the same time it is becoming spiritually the darkest time as Satan is letting out all stops.

Thank you Jake Friesen for seeking with all your heart the prophetic word of the Lord so that the Kingdom of God will triumph over the kingdom of darkness!

Blayne Greiner

Director, Youth Unlimited
International Speaker and Trainer
Youth Minister

For over fifty years I have listened to the voices of the prophets, especially pertaining to the all consuming subject of Christ's Second Coming. I was converted to Christ at the age of eleven, but at the age of 17, I had in effect a second conversion in the sense of becoming aware of God's purposes for Israel in the last days of the present age. It so happened that in my Grade 12 Class, in the Spring of 1948, I was given an assignment to write about Palestine, and in the process, I sensed that with Israel's returning to nationhood after a 2000 year dispersion, we were witnessing prophetic truth being fulfilled before our very eyes.

In the meantime, I have accumulated and read some 100 books in my personal library on the subject of eschatology. I have likely been subjected to all the variations of interpretation that you have, including dispensational dogmatism, date-setting, pre-tribulation versus post-tribulation positions, etc.

In my own denominational background, I have decried the fact that while some fifty years ago, leading

❖

Forward

figures in our churches had much to say about the Lord's Return and would conduct entire weekend seminars on the subject, with a great deal of public interest, today, these many years later, our churches have become virtually silent on the matter. I believe this silence holds true across most of the evangelical spectrum of churches today.

While I have been engaged in a variety of ministries over the years, this overriding concern about end-time truth continued to resurface for me again and again. Where I have had opportunity to share along these lines, I have sought to do so, and I have sensed a hunger in the hearts of God's people to know about these things. Many times, over the years, as I waited upon the Lord in personal prayer retreats, I have labored under the passion that I too should speak a more definitive word for God on this issue. Hence this booklet.

My prayer is that in the process, God's people might both be encouraged and prepared for all that lies ahead in the coming days.

The burden of what I share in this presentation is Scripture itself, and my understanding of it; I do refer to a number of other book sources as well, and these will be listed in the bibliography at the end of this volume.

Regarding the title, The Seer, I do not claim that title for myself, but I do believe there is a call to the church of our day for renewed spiritual sight and awareness.

Jake H. Friesen

A physicist by the name of Fred Singer, made the facetious comment: "Prediction is a very difficult business, particularly about the future." Truly we need a good dose of modesty in dealing with any prophetic themes.

Introduction

The original idea of a title for this book was: Prophetic Perspective #2007. Since book titles can help to catch the reader's attention, I thought the number 2007 might have caused you to take a second look! There is a reason for this number, which I refer to in a later chapter. On the other hand, I am also trying to poke fun at some of our preoccupation with dates, which is precisely what the Lord warned us against. I also think we sometimes take ourselves too seriously in prophetic areas, and it is time we confessed to more of our humanness in understanding and interpretation of God's truth.

But seriously, why another perspective, when so much has been written and spoken? First, for myself, if God mandates another statement, I want to obey His prompting.

Second, prophetic utterances in some way resemble computers, of which it has been said that as soon as you buy one, it is out of date. This calls for ongoing messages to be given even as our times change.

Third, I have questioned the tone of some of the material I've seen. There has been a lot of dogmatism, for instance, on minor matters. There is often a lack of humility about things that we can't really be sure about. We see strong opinions on one particular interpretation, and judgmental responses on others with differing views. I remember John Wimber, the founder of the Vineyard movement saying on one occasion: "The only word God has pledged to honor is His own!"

Fourth, the majority of what is written and preached today reflects a strong pre-tribulation rapture position, which I consider one sided, and hazardous for the body of Christ entering difficult times.

Fifth, given the forwardness of secular media and tabloids to speak out about futuristic themes, is it not in order that the church speak out on what God has said on the subject?

Sixth, the world has changed since September 11, 2001. For the first time in her history, mainland America has been attacked by enemy forces on her own soil, using her own resources as weapons. There has been an ongoing awareness since then that we are not as secure as we thought we were, and perhaps the time has come to review our spiritual weaponry as well.

There is an intriguing Scripture in Psalm 103:7: *'He made known His ways to Moses, His acts to the children of Israel.'* The people saw the acts of God, but Moses, the Seer of God, saw beyond the acts into the ways and thoughts of God. All of us saw the horrendous acts of September 11. Have we been able to hear what God was saying to us through these events?

Let me add a word about the title, The Seer. This title is given to the prophetic office in Scripture, and is used at least 28 times. It is easy for us to see the unregenerate world as blind to the truth of the gospel, which to many is so obvious and illuminating. When Jesus commissioned Paul to the ministry of preaching to the unsaved, He spoke of the gospel:

> *...opening their eyes and turning them from darkness to light, and from the power of Satan to God, that they may receive forgiveness of sins and an inheritance...*
>
> - Acts 26:18

It is relatively easy for those of us in the Christian church to see the blindness of Israel regarding Jesus the Messiah. Paul concurs with this blindness and says:

> *God has given them a spirit of stupor, eyes that they should not see, and ears that they should not hear...*
>
> - Romans 11:8

What is difficult for us to understand is that the church itself should be blind. Did Jesus not designate us as the light of the world? (Matthew 5:14). In his letter to the Laodicean church, Revelation chapter three, the Lord says to this church:

> Because you say, 'I am rich, have become wealthy, and have need of nothing'---and do not know that you are wretched, miserable, poor, blind and naked---I counsel you to...anoint your eyes with eye salve, that you may see.
>
> - Revelation 3:17,18.

God has given prophets to His people throughout the ages, to declare His truth and to see beyond the present. They were to be the spiritual watchmen on the walls, warning of any danger in the distance. But if seers no longer see, the people of God are exposed to the enemy. *'Who is blind but my servant?'* cries Isaiah in chapter 42:19. Blind prophets are an oxymoron. When the salt has lost its savor, it not only becomes useless but it is misleading.

God not only gave prophets in the Old Covenant, He gave a prophetic voice to the New Testament church. See Ephesians 4:11, where a five fold ministry is outlined, including that of the prophet. Unfortunately, this office has been poorly understood, often abused, and not properly encouraged when it does emerge.

It is said of the children of Issachar in the times of David, that they had *'understanding of the times, to know what Israel ought to do'*. I do not think that God wants His people to enter the great challenges of the days ahead blind folded. God has never allowed major crises to come without due warning.

God has also provided seers for our times. May we be like the men of Issachar, understanding the times, and hearing from God what it is He wants us to do.

We are told that one quarter to one third of Scripture is prophetic. In terms of the books of the Bible, we have a recognized prophetic section in the Old Testament, consisting of 17 books, and in the New Testament, the book of Revelation. Thus in terms of these 18 books out of the 66 of our Canon, we count over 27% as being prophetic.

Analyzing the very content of the verses of Scripture, let me quote from J.Barton Payne: "Out of the Old Testament's 23,210 verses, 6,641 contain predictive material, or 29%. Out of the New Testament's 7,914 verses, 1,711 contain predictive material, or 22%. So for the entire Bible's 31,124 verses, 8,352 contain predictive material, or 27% of the whole Bible."

This begs the question among others, is there a proportionate emphasis in our Bible teaching and Bible preaching of prophetic truth?

When I was 14, and a young Christian, my parents gave me a Bible for Christmas, called "The Marked Bible". It covered all of Scripture

Chapter 1

Prophetic Preoccupation of Scripture

with four great themes, one of the four being prophetic, and then proceeded to color in purple all the verses of 19 prophetic sub-themes, and again, these verses ran the gamut from Genesis to Revelation.

There is so much more prophetic content throughout Scripture than meets the eye. The Psalms particularly are filled with prophetic nuggets. I have a book in my library entitled, "Hidden Prophecies in the Psalms", by J.R.Church, and I have been intrigued by these truths for many years. Psalm Two, for instance, is one of the most graphic illustrations of Armageddon to come. Psalm 46 is a great testimonial to God's faithfulness to His people when the world around them is falling apart. Psalm 37 is a reminder of God's provision for His people in times of hunger and crisis. Psalm 91 speaks of dramatic divine protection for God's people in the midst of surrounding chaos.

Jesus Christ, the Son of God, our blessed Savior, was Himself the Prophet that the Old Testament had predicted that was to come, *'a Prophet...like unto me (Moses)'* (Deuteronomy 18:15, Acts 3:22). Prophetic nuggets are to be found throughout the gospels in the sayings of Jesus. However, it is in the Olivet Discourse that Jesus particularly focuses on the Last Days in answer to the question of the disciples.

There comes that moment in the life of a teacher when a pupil asks the question the teacher has longed to expound on. The Olivet Discourse, found in Matthew 24-25, appeared to be that kind of a moment. Imagine the group of disciples sitting there, overlooking the Temple, the city of Jerusalem, and to have the Christ expound on its future, affecting as it would, all of history. So Jesus, on this particular occasion, takes these two long chapters in Matthew to answer the questions, When will these things be? What will be the sign of your coming, and of the end of the age? (Matthew 24:3). The other Synoptic gospels, Mark and Luke, also convey similar messages, and add various detail. It has been my stance for years, that the prophetic words Jesus the Prophet spoke, should be the template through which all other prophetic utterances should be interpreted.

In the above text, Matthew 24:3 in the old King James version speaks of the end of the world, but the New King James correctly states end of the age. The world will not end, but this age will come to an end. The proverbial toilet roll is a picture of seemingly endless cycles which finally finishes. Our earthly lives continue in seemingly endless cycles of days and weeks and years, but there comes a day when we walk our last walk, and eat our last meal, and breathe our last breath. These are graphic reminders of our present age, and when the disciples asked the question, Jesus did not ignore it, but addressed it fully in these two great chapters of Matthew.

Prophetic truths permeate the New Testament, and Paul who was instrumental in establishing so many of the early churches, took pains to enlighten his flock about the Lord's Return. Some of the obvious passages include First and Second Thessalonians, and First Corinthians 15, the great Resurrection chapter.

It was Peter, the spokesman for the original Twelve, who declares in his second book:

We also have the prophetic word made more sure,
which you do well to heed as a light that shines in a
dark place, until the day dawns and the morning star
rises in your hearts...

The one official prophetic book of the New Testament is the book of Revelation. One of the common errors is to pluralize the name, whereas its singular title fits well with the idea that it is the revelation about Christ and by Christ (Revelation 1:1), rather than a series of difficult images about a dismal future.

One of the great statements in this book is found in chapter 19 verse 10: *'For the testimony of Jesus is the spirit of prophecy.'* I have pondered this statement for a long time. It speaks to me of the fact that prophetic truth is centered in Jesus Christ, and that is significant in a world that desires to know its future without the person of Christ. We need to affirm that all prophetic utterances even in Scripture are merely side-plays of kingdoms come and gone compared to that Prophetic Word about The Prophet to come. It is His kingdom that, like a Rock without hands, (Daniel 2) descends to crush all other kingdoms and establish the reign of Christ as our only true Sovereign, King of kings and Lord of lords. Hallelujah!

It is noteworthy that the book of Revelation is the only book that begins with a specific blessing for the reader:

Blessed is he who reads and those who hear the
words of this prophecy, and keep those things which
are written in it; for the time is near.

- Revelations 1:3

I have done this literally with a Bible Study Care Group, reading through the entire book out loud with stops here and there for questions and comments. While so much of the meaning of that difficult middle part of the book has remained elusive and even fearful, there is no question in my mind that the time of fulfillment yet to come will bring about new understanding and appreciation for its message.

Not only is a large part of Scripture taken up with the prophetic; a large part of that prophetic material has to do with the Last Days of the age. I have a statement to the effect that there are 20 times as many references in the Old Testament to Christ's Second Coming as there are for the First. According to my sources there are 44 references for the First, so that makes some 880 for the Second. Also, we are told that one of every 30 verses in the New Testament points to the Second Coming. This would involve some 265 verses. Adding 880 to the 265 would make 1145 verses in Scripture referring to Christ's Return.

It is impressive that in the Old Testament prophetic Scripture, the prophets of that day speak out to decadent Israel, and to the issues of their day; yet, by the Spirit of God, they are carried beyond the issues of their times, to the End of times, when Messiah would come and restore all things.

The great hymns of the church, echoing our theology and our faith, reflect the hope and longing for Christ's return. Many hymns are totally given to this great truth. Take a typical hymn, and invariably you will find one verse out of three or four devoted to the blessed hope of His Coming.

Billy Graham mentioned that of Charles Wesley's 7000 hymns, 5000 spoke of the Second Coming of Christ.

In this spirit Paul, having spoken of Jewish history, declares:

> *Now all these things happened to them as examples, and they were written for our admonition, on whom the ends of the world have come.*
>
> - 1 Corinthians 10:11

We might declare, on the strength of this statement, that while the Bible was written for all ages, it was written also especially for the last generation that would witness the final fulfillment of all that was to take place. Flying to Atlanta one day, and viewing the chart of incoming flights into that busy Airport, one of the busiest in the country, reminded me again of 1 Corinthians 10:11, and how the many prophetic utterances of all the centuries will finally merge in one grand finale in the Day of the Lord.

The role of prophecy also raises the question of how prophetic truth impacts people's lives. It is extremely important to understand that prophetic truth in Scripture is always given with the implication of responsive and responsible life styles. Peter in his second book, speaking of the end of the age, asks the question that all of us need to be asking, *'Therefore...what manner of persons ought you to be?'* (2 Peter 3:11). This question deserves a broader answer and is discussed further in chapter 10.

Why is it that the whole subject of prophecy, including the prophetic truth of Scripture, is so neglected, even shunned and resisted by evangelical Christians? Is it because so much of false dogmatism, mentioned earlier? Is it because of fear of doomsday scenarios? Is it because we have heard so many divergent opinions from supposed experts, we don't know what to believe? Is it because we have been affected by our culture that promotes the good life, and doesn't want to hear any bad news that might threaten our life styles? Could it also be that the enemy, knowing the time is near, would seek to keep God's people from being as aware and prepared as they were intended to be?

It is a bold thing for any generation to consider their generation the last. But of course there comes a time when that becomes true! History does not repeat itself endlessly, but there is an End, which Jesus referred to repeatedly, see Matthew 24, for example. If we should be that end time generation, and if the Lord had given us the intelligence and data whereby we might know that this were true, and if then we failed to be aware of that reality, would this not be a tragedy? This begs the question of times and seasons versus dates, which is the theme of our next chapter.

Ought we to set dates for the Lord's Return? The answer is clearly No.

Ought we to be aware of Times and Seasons? The answer from the Scriptures is clearly Yes.

Yet I find people implying that because we are not to set dates, that we need not concern ourselves with the seasons either. It is the Lord who gave us instructions on both counts, and it is He Who calls us to a balanced approach.

Let us review a few pertinent texts, warning us about date setting:

No one knows the day or the hour.
- Matthew 24:36

You don't know the hour.
- Matthew 24:42

You don't know the day or the hour.
- Matthew 25:13

No one knows the day or the hour...not even the Son, but the Father.
- Mark 13:32-37

Chapter 2

Times & Seasons vs. Dates

One recent date setter, whose book I have in my collection, wrote in 1988, *88 reasons why Christ will return in 1988.* When that didn't happen, he wrote another, *89 reasons why...* You can fill in the blanks. Some people don't give up easily.

But what about the seasons? 1 Thessalonians 5:1 states *'Regarding times and seasons, there is no need to write you...for you know...'* In Matthew 16:1-3, Jesus comments on the keenness with which the religious leaders of Israel discerned the weather. He concludes, verse 3, saying, *'Hypocrites! You know how to discern the face of the sky, but you cannot discern the signs of the times?'*

When the disciples asked Jesus about the signs of His Coming and of the end of the age, He did not dismiss these questions as irrelevant, but spends two chapters (Matthew 24, 25) in answering their queries. In the very same chapters where he speaks out against setting dates, he nevertheless gives some pertinent information which will prepare His people for those last days of the age.

It is exciting to think that God is Alpha and Omega, the beginning and the ending, the First and the Last, and to Him the future is more obvious than yesterday is to us. It is also exciting that God has chosen to reveal to His people His plans for the future. Is it not appropriate that one should search out all that God has chosen to reveal, even as someone in receipt of an inheritance would apply every resource to obtain and maximize that which has been bequeathed to him?

If God indeed has revealed the future in His Book, and if there is such a thing as the end of the age, and if we come to that generation, and that generation should be quite ignorant of what was happening, would that not be a major tragedy?

We have instances of rebuke because people were willfully ignorant of God's workings. In Luke 19:44, Jesus cries over Jerusalem, *'because thou knewest not the time of thy visitation.'* Asaph, in Psalm 74, decries the lack of vision: *'We do not see our signs, there is no longer any prophet; nor is there any among us who knows how long. O God, how long will the adversary reproach?'* Jeremiah complains:

> *Even the stork in the heavens knows her appointed times; and the turtledove, the swift, and the swallow observe the time of their coming. But My People do not know the judgment of the Lord.*
>
> - Jeremiah 8:7

Let me share some more Scripture that speak to God's desire to reveal to his servants what He is planning to do.

Approaching the judgment of Sodom and Gomorrah, Genesis 18, the Lord says, *'Shall I hide from Abraham what I am doing...?'* That led to a dialogue about the pending event, and intercession which had the potential of averting catastrophe.

> *Surely the Lord God does nothing, unless He reveals His secret to His servants the prophets. A lion has roared! Who will not fear? The Lord God has spoken! Who can but prophesy?*
>
> - Amos 3:7-8

11

Ask Me of things to come!

- Isaiah 45:11

The Spirit of Truth...will show you things to come.

- John 16:13

...(we are) stewards of the mysteries of God.

- 1 Corinthians 4:1

It is given unto you to know the mysteries of the kingdom of heaven.

- Matthew 13:11

*Eye has not seen...the things God has prepared...**but God has revealed them to us by His Spirit.***

- 1 Corinthians 2:9-12

*Behold the former things have come to pass, and new things I declare; **before they spring forth I tell you of them.***

- Isaiah 42:9

Call to Me, and I will answer you, and show you great and mighty things, which you do not know.

- Jeremiah 33:3

The secret things belong unto the Lord our God, but those things which are revealed belong unto us and to our children for ever, that we may do all the words of this law.

- Deuteronomy 29:29

I will stand upon my watch...and see what He will
say to me...And the Lord answered, Write the
vision...that he may run that reads it...

- Habakkuk 2:1-3

The secret of the Lord is with those who fear Him,
and He will show them His covenant.

- Psalm 25:14

We note occasions where men in tune with God knew that
prophetic history was unfolding before them. Peter's statement on the Day of Pentecost is a case in point.

Defending the actions of the believers before the critics of
the day who supposed them to be drunk, Peter referred to
the outpouring of the Spirit predicted by the prophet Joel,
and declared, *'this is that!'* (Acts 2:16).

I have heard several accounts stating that no believers were
caught up in the great destruction of Jerusalem by Titus in
70 A.D. because they had heeded the words of Jesus according to Luke 21:20-21 that *'when you see Jerusalem sur-*
rounded by armies...then let those in Judea flee to the
mountains...' They saw the signal, they obeyed the prophetic word, and they saved their lives, while many thousands in the city perished.

If ever there was a time that God wanted His people to be
knowledgeable about end time events, would it not be at the
end of the age? The writer to the Hebrews speaks of believers in the anticipation of the Lord's Return *'exhorting one*
another, and so much the more as you see the Day
approaching.' (Hebrews 10:25).

Daniel was distinctly told that God was sealing up the prophetic message *'till the time of the end'* (Daniel 12:9). It is
interesting that the book of Revelation is an account of the
great unsealing, as Jesus the Lamb opens the seven sealed
book to reveal to God's people the events of the last days
(Revelation 5).

Speaking of Daniel, it is also noteworthy, that God's people
of the end times are characterized as people of wisdom.

> *None of the wicked shall understand, but the wise
> shall understand.*
>
> - Daniel 12:10

> *Those who are wise shall shine like the brightness of
> the firmament.*
>
> - Daniel 12:3

> *Seal the book till the time of the end...**knowledge
> shall increase.***
>
> - Daniel 12:4

> *The people who know their God shall be strong, and
> carry out great exploits.*
>
> - Daniel 11:32

This challenge toward wisdom is also reflected in Jesus'
story of the ten virgins, five of which were wise, and five,
foolish (Matthew 25:1-13). It is also reflected in the stories
of the wise man versus the foolish man with houses built on
a foundation of rock versus sand (Matthew 7:24-27).

If indeed we are to be knowledgeable about the day in which we live, what are the indicators that we might be that last generation that the Bible speaks about?

When the disciples asked about signs, Jesus spoke about signs, and we wish to deal with these in due course. But first of all he spoke about phenomena that would happen, but these would not yet point to the end, things like earthquakes and pestilences.

Admittedly, these kinds of events have always been with us, so how can they in themselves be signs?

The first time he speaks about the end happening in this chapter is in verse 14:

...this gospel of the kingdom will be preached in all the world as a witness to all the nations, and then the end will come.

This text is often cited as a missionary text, to the effect that the better we do the job of world evangelization, the sooner the Lord will come. While the task of world missions is our God given responsibility, according to the Great Commission, this is not exactly the thrust of what Jesus is saying here, as I read it. This verse is not a command to preach, so much as it is a reflection on the preaching having happened. There is more to the sovereignty of God as to how world evangelization will happen and to assess when the job is done. God will use any and every means He pleases to get His message of the gospel so that every one will know the truth. God will even send troubled times to cause men to call upon the name of the Lord (Acts 2:17-21).

The ministry of Billy Graham is a great example of evangelism in our day. I have just read several books by and about him. It is probably no exaggeration to say that he has preached the gospel to more people in one generation than any predecessor. He has preached the gospel on every continent. He has visited most countries in the world, including places like Russia, China and North Korea. He has spent time with heads of state all over the world, and has personally related to all the current presidents of the United States. After seeing God's blessing on the Crusade meetings early in his ministry, he started a radio program, at first reluctantly. It became known as the Hour of Decision. He has used Television, a vehicle that had become available to our generation for the first time in history. He used the printed page in various formats: Decision magazine for the average reader, and Christianity Today for the academic and the theologian. Many films were produced by World Wide Pictures, telling a graphic story and bringing people head to head with the gospel message through Billy Graham. In later years, Billy Graham has sponsored a series of major conferences where thousands of native evangelists from third world countries could come together to learn, to be equipped to go back to their own countries to do the job of evangelism even more effectively. Several of these were held in Amsterdam, Holland in the 1980's.

Surely the story of this one man, whom God has given to our generation, is a major contribution to achieve God's purposes to have the gospel preached to every creature before Jesus returns.

John Wesley White, from Ontario, one of Billy Graham's associate evangelists, has issued a White Paper, relating current events to Scripture. In one of these he mentions a Dr. Sam Thielman, son of Billy Graham's pastor, who is a psychiatrist, having attended a conference at Harvard with 7000 psychiatrists present, where a professor gave a spell binding report of evangelism in our day. "There is an out-pouring of the Spirit in the world today" he said. He mentioned that in the past 90 years, the world's population of charismatic Christians had grown to half a billion. He spoke of half a million believers being martyred for their faith in 1998 alone. He stated that in the Chinese underground church alone, there had been one hundred million Christian rebirths in one generation. Finally he added that in the third world over one hundred thousand people are born again every single day!

One of the books I've found helpful in recent years is by Rick Joyner, titled "The Harvest". I came away from that reading with a renewed sense that the greatest harvest of all times was yet to come, at the end of the age. In the context of the parable of the wheat and the tares, Jesus says, *'the harvest is the end of the age'* (Matthew 13:39).

People sometimes say that with the world being so evil, how can God claim the victory over the souls of men if so many are lost. Again, the harvest comes at the end of the age, and it is not until the harvest is in, that we can make a proper evaluation of the crop. Harvest time is an exciting time to look forward to, not only from the vantage point of the spiritual returns, but also from the vantage point of the instruments that God is preparing even now to bring in the harvest.

The crop of tares speaks to the culminating harvest of evil at the end of the age, but wheat speaks to the harvest of good. God is the superintendent of both. Jesus said, *'My Father is the vinedresser'* (John 15:1).

Whatever we make of signs, we must never forget that above and beyond any crises that may yet lie ahead, God's people are not to fear, but rather rejoice because their redemption draws near, and because the Lord of redemption is even now at work in the hearts of people all over the world.

Having said all these things about the great theme of evangelism, I would still like to say that this is not the direct answer of Jesus as to what constitute signs. I wish to deal more specifically with that question in the next chapter.

There are many prophetic messages given out these days, and you can even access them by computer on the Internet. Concerning prophecies Paul says in 1 Thessalonians 5:19-21, *'Do not quench the Spirit. Do not despise prophecies. Test all things; hold fast what is good.'* What wise advice for our day. We need the balance of not despising, but on the other hand discerning what is being said. I have learned to respect the ministry of a brother David Damien, who has undertaken a spiritual mantle of intercession for Canada, and works with an organization called, Watchmen for the

Nations. A prophetic word was given by another brother Emile Abadir in this organization on March 27, 1999, in which he stated, among other things that "the next five years will witness a turning point in the history of all mankind." This kind of time projection coincides with a number of other sober commentaries that have come my way recently.

Some time ago, I prepared a "What If..." statement that speaks to the question of where we are in history, and I would like to include it here.

What If...

There has been a popular concept of history repeating itself.

What if in contrast to this mind set, there were a *word*, a reliable messenger, that speaks to a linear view, pointing to the *end* of the age? (We believe the Holy Scripture is such a *word*) (Matthew 24:3)

What if in the context of such a *word*, there is a strong ingredient called *prophecy*, which we are instructed to heed (but which most Christians precisely tend to ignore and avoid)? (2 Peter 1:19-21)

What if in the context of such a *prophetic word*, a *sign* were given, that would point to the ushering in of the end of the age? (We would consider Israel to be that sign, the Fig Tree of Matthew 24).

What if we should be living in the time frame when this and accompanying signs occur? (I was 17 when Israel became a nation after nearly 2000 years of dispersion)

What if I were born at such a time that I could reasonably expect not only to see the Signs, but also the fulfilment of the Second Coming in my life time? (I was born in 1931) What is the meaning of, This generation shall not pass? (Matthew 24:34)

What if there were contained in the prophetic Word a concept of a day equaling a 1000 years, which have been pictured by Jewish rabbis for centuries as a pattern of six 1000- year- days of human labor, culminating in a 7th day of divine rest? (See Psalm 90:4 and 2 Peter 3:8). What if that should leave us at the twilight of day Six, and the dawning of a new day of righteousness?

What if on the one hand it is often the fanatical fringe, even in the secular media, which speaks of the end of the age (world), whereas most mainline churches, even Evangelical, display 'business as usual' approaches? The latter ridicule the 'hype' mentality of the former and thereby feel even more justified in their stance. What if in their sophisticated blindness many could miss the posted warning signs God has given us?

What if half of Christendom were divided against Israel, with the other half showing repentance for our wrongs with love and support for Israel?

What if the first half that were indifferent to Israel's role in God's plan, thereby should miss God's major *sign* for the end of the age?

Most believers would concur with #1 above. By the same token, most believers would be in ignorance about *all the others*! Christians readily admit to the blindness that has happened to Israel regarding Messiah; is there not a comparable blindness that has befallen the church?

The Seer

The religious leaders of Israel asked for a sign, and were rebuffed by Jesus because of their unspiritual motives. (Matthew 16:1-4) On the other hand, when the disciples asked for a sign, Jesus spent two chapters answering their questions. (Matthew 24 and 25)

To quote what the disciples asked for, see Matthew 24, verses one to three.

Chapter 3

The Signs of Israel and Jerusalem

Jesus had predicted the destruction of the temple which seemed so incomprehensible to these Jewish disciples. So they asked him privately,

1. Tell us, when will these things be?
2. What will be the sign of your Coming,
3. And [the sign] of the end of the age?

Jesus used the opportunity of these enquiries, to address not only the immediate tragedy that would befall the city and the temple, but to speak to the larger subject of His Coming at the end of the age.

In the next verses Jesus speaks to various phenomena that shall occur, of which he says, *'the end is not yet'* (verse 6). It is interesting and potentially misleading that we so often read into Scripture, and especially prophetic Scripture, things we want to see.

How often these phenomena, including wars, pestilences and earthquakes, have been touted as signs of Christ's near return. In a sense, Jesus is saying just the opposite.

These are the kinds of events that often create panic and hysteria about the world coming to an end. So Jesus is saying that these things are *not* the end.

The reality is that these kinds of phenomena have plagued parts of the world throughout the centuries, but the world did not end. When we come to Jesus' answer regarding the sign we are to look for, these phenomena also play a part, but they must be seen in the context of the larger picture. When Christ's time for the end comes, these phenomena will mark the beginning of sorrows (verse 8), or the beginning of birth pangs, which must eventually lead to the birthing of God's new order for His world. (See Matthew 19:28)

In the first 14 verses of Matthew 24, the word *end* occurs three times, in verses 6, 13, and 14. Only in verse 14 does he speak to an indicator of the end coming, referring to the world wide proclamation of the gospel.

We already touched on verse 14 in the previous chapter. Allow me to share a few additional thoughts here. With all due respect to every genuine missionary endeavor, the text does not say that our actions will precipitate Christ's return. I believe, as a dear father in Christ shared years ago, that when all is said and done, we will see examples of how God sovereignly penetrated heathen fortresses that no missions committee could have planned. I believe that part of the fulfillment of this text will include the powerful witness of the Jewish nation, that have yet to find Jesus as Messiah. It will include the testimony of the two witnesses mentioned in Revelation 11. These two witnesses probably includes the powerful ministry of Elijah, who shall *'turn the hearts of the fathers to the children'* according to the last chapter of the Old Testament. It will even include the unconventional flying angel of Revelation 14:6, *'having the everlasting gospel to preach to those who dwell on the earth-to every nation, tribe, tongue, and people...'* All these are just the bare bones of another subject, but fascinating indeed.

But to return to the Matthew text: the whole point of giving a sign means that it must be seen. The first time the word *see* is used in Jesus' answer is in verse 15, and he speaks here of the *'abomination of desolation'*, and he is quoting from Daniel, who spoke so specifically to the end of the age those hundreds of years earlier.

The seeing of this sign, of the abomination of desolation, of which more will be said in the next chapter, is such an obvious event, unlike earthquakes or famine, occurring as it will in a specific landmark (temple) in a recognized city (Jerusalem) in the land of Judea, Israel, that no one could misread it.

This sign has yet to occur, for while there is a restored Israel, and while Jerusalem has returned to Jewish authority after thousands of years, there is still no temple at the time of this writing in 2002.

In the meantime, the fact of the restoration of Israel after centuries of Jewish dispersion all over the globe becomes *the context* for everything else in the chapter.

Having brought us to the great subject of His coming, verse 31, more of which we will deal with later, He makes this grand summary statement, verse 32, Now learn this parable from the fig tree...and He goes on to talk about the leaves forming. Again, there is something to see, *'When you see all these things, know that He is near...'* verse 33.

Compare this also Luke 21:29-31, where seeing is mentioned in each of these verses:

> *Look at the fig tree, and all the trees. When they are already budding, you see and know for yourselves that summer is now near. So likewise, when you see these things happening, know that the kingdom of God is near.*

I believe the fig tree is Israel, and I say this for several reasons. Firstly, Israel is symbolized by various trees including the fig tree in several Scriptures including Joel 1:7.

Secondly, the fig tree had just figured in Jesus' and the disciples' week, where the fig tree that bore no fruit had been cursed by Jesus, see Matthew 21:18-22. The Pulpit Commentary speaks to this and says in effect that to attribute Jesus' reaction to the fruitless fig tree as a temper tantrum is preposterous; that the only viable explanation of his words is a prophetic statement about the nation. Thus we have a nation at 30 A.D. still carrying the outward form (leaves) but without fruit (faith). In short order even that outward form would be destroyed (this happened at 70 A.D. with the destruction of Jerusalem under the Roman general Titus). Then in future times, when God would once again restore the form (allow the nation to re-emerge, yet without faith), that would be the indication that His Coming was near. *'So you also, when you see all these things, know that He is near, at the very doors.'* (Matthew 24:33).

If someone questions whether the fig tree is Israel, the counter question must be asked, What else could the fig tree mean? I have not heard of a viable alternative.

The generation that shall not pass away, verse 34, has been interpreted in various ways. Evaluating what I have read, I feel that it is at least an optional interpretation to say that the generation living at the time of the sign given will see the fulfillment of Jesus' Return. If this is true, this still begs several questions: How long is a generation? What specific sign marks the beginning of the generation time frame?

If Israel's rebirth (1948) marks the beginning of a generation, and a generation is 40 years, as has often been said, Jesus should have returned in 1988. We know that didn't happen, and here already we have cause for humility and caution.

God's focus, however, is not only on the land, Israel, but also on the city, Jerusalem, and on the Temple.

I have gleaned the following from Jack van Impe, whom I appreciate for the fact that He keeps reminding us of God's prophetic calendar. He reported having come to a new insight about the city being a critical factor in God's time table. That began to make sense to me as I went back to Daniel 9 and the Seventy Weeks Prophecy, which centers around the city: *'Seventy weeks are determined for your people and for Your Holy City....'* (Daniel 9:24) Could it be that God counts time from the critical events of the city, and this could also apply to the generation statement of Matthew 24?

The falling of Jerusalem into Jewish hands after nearly 2000 years on June 6, 1967, was certainly an event not only of historical, but also prophetic import. Even Billy Graham commented on this, and spoke of that day as a fulfillment of the words of Jesus in Luke 21:24, *'Jerusalem shall be trampled by Gentiles until the times of the gentiles are fulfilled.'*

Might this indicate that the Lord started a divine Countdown from that day forward, and that His Coming now is very near, even at the doors?

Certainly it is appropriate that we pray along with the very last prayer of the Bible in the book of Revelation, *'Even so come, Lord Jesus!'* (Revelation 22: 20)

Probably the most powerful prophetic time line in Scripture is given us by Daniel in chapter nine, already referred to in this chapter, and referred to by Jesus Himself in Matthew 24. This text of Daniel forms the theme of our next chapter.

Permit me to add a few further foot notes here to the subject of Israel in the prophetic calendar. I had facetiously chosen as the original title for this booklet, *Prophetic Perspectives 2007*, as mentioned earlier, and that was based on adding a forty year generation to the year 1967 when Jerusalem fell into Jewish hands. This is exactly the kind of date setting we need to stay away from, even though we may be aware that the end is approaching.

That God should choose the Jewish nation as a sign of His unfolding calendar is part of His eternal sovereign plan. He had already chosen this nation to be the instruments of His divine revelation, the Holy Scriptures. They were also the people from whom Messiah would come. That Israel even survived after the horrific events of 70 A.D. and her subsequent dispersion into all nations is a major miracle. That Israel should then return to her own land after two thousand years of exile is not only a further miracle; it is unparalleled in all the annals of history. At no time has another people lost its own country for two thousand years, and then returned to reclaim it.

Reading from Isaiah 11, there is a reference to the Root of Jesse being a banner (verse 10) and certainly Christ was a sign to be recognized or spoken against, Luke 2:34; but it also refers to the gathering of Israel in the end times as a banner for the nations, verse 12. Is there a good reason why the tiny nation of Israel and the city of Jerusalem should be so central to the current events of the day, totally out of proportion to their size and population, were it not for the fact that this country and this city are a strategic part of a spiritual end times drama between the forces of light and darkness? In this context one reads of Jerusalem becoming a cup of drunkenness and a heavy stone for all those who seek to shape its destiny for their own ends. See Zechariah 12:1-3.

The church, of course, has been preoccupied with various and contradictory approaches to Israel as a prophetic entity. It has been popular in many evangelical circles to think of the church itself as the new spiritual Israel, leaving no room for the original Jewish nation, or her restoration to her land as having any prophetic significance. Among the notable men of God who have spoken to the significance of the restoration of the nation to its land is none other than Charles Haddon Spurgeon (1834-92), the great Baptist preacher of the 19th century in England. His life and ministry predated Israel's return by many years. I have with me a 13 page document issued by Dennis M. Swanson, Head Librarian and Director of Israel Studies, The Master's Seminary, Sun Valley, California, which details Spurgeon's statements on Israel's return to the land, referring especially to a sermon given at the Metropolitan Tabernacle in 1864.

His views include the concepts of Israel as a nation coming to faith in Christ; the restoration of national identity, and a return to the Promised Land, with the parameters of that land corresponding to the promises given Abraham and David.

Speaking of Abraham, we should be reminded of God's repeated and unconditional promises to Abraham about the land. I do not know of any other piece of real estate so divinely given. Could this be the reason for this very area being so hotly contested in our very day?

In Genesis 12:1, God says to Abraham, *'Get out of your country...to a land that I will show you.'* In verse seven He says, *'To your descendants I will give this land.'* In chapter 13, after the contest with nephew Lot, God reinforces the promise, verses 14-17, *'Lift your eyes now, and look from the place where you are-northward, southward, eastward, and westward; for all the land which you see I give to you and your descendants forever....Arise, walk in the land through its length and its width, for I give it to you.'* Chapter 15:7, God says, *'I am the Lord, who brought you out of Ur of the Chaldeans, to give you this land to inherit it.'* More references continue in Genesis 15:18-21, with specific borders mentioned, and again in chapter 17:8.

Joan Peters has written a well documented book entitled, *From Time Immemorial,* in which she examines the Arab and Jewish historical claims to the land of Israel, and in her research and personal investigations, she discovered that a lot of what is perpetrated in our day by the media is myth rather than fact. Non Jewish claimants to the land "from time immemorial" cannot be substantiated.

If we believe in the restoration of Israel nationally and spiritually, one might ask, which comes first? It seems to me that Jesus' comments in Matthew 24 of the fig tree, would indicate an entry without spiritual fruit, but with the fruit coming later. We visited Israel twice, once in 1983, and again in 1985. I recorded many impressions at the time, and one of the questions I asked myself: If God would have restored His people to the land, which would be the greater miracle, to restore them sighted, or blind? The answer is obviously the latter. The flip side of course is, that if the *blind* re entry has brought about such amazing changes to the land and to the various levels of restored nationhood, how much more will be accomplished for the Kingdom of God, when the full restoration is realized! Romans 9-11 is apropos here, especially 11:15: *'for if their being cast away is the reconciling of the world, what will their acceptance be but life from the dead!'* The spiritual turning of Israel can only be compared to a resurrection which will not only impact the nation, but make them into flaming evangelists which will impact the world.

I mentioned briefly in the Forward that I had undergone a kind of second spiritual conversion in the Spring of 1948, where I sensed that God was fulfilling prophetic history before our eyes, by allowing the Jewish people to be restored to nationhood and to their land. Throughout all the years of my life and ministry since I have had this burning passion for Israel, and God's purposes for them and through them. Many of my friends do not necessarily share that kind of passion, and I think it is good that we have grace to listen to each other. At this point I also pray for your indulgence as I seek to share some of the things God has laid on my heart.

If it is hard to believe that the present Israel has any spiritual potential for the Kingdom of God, it may be helpful to remember that Old Testament Israel often faded into a spiritual back water. I often found it difficult to even think of a king like Ahab being part of God's people, seeing as he sold himself to wickedness, along with his wife Jezebel. It was at this very time of moral decadence on the part of the nation and many of its leaders, that God raised up the great prophets who spoke to the issues of the day, but then also reminded the people that God's purposes were not yet fulfilled. It is in the context of God's plans for Israel that Paul states, *'the gifts and the calling of God are irrevocable.'* Romans 11:29.

There is an interesting reference in the book of the prophet Ezekiel chapter 38, and verse 12, speaking of Israel in the midst of the land. That word midst can be understood as navel, the place where the umbilical cord is attached to the newborn child. If we think of God as the Father/Mother of Israel, we might say that the tiny land of Israel is God's special attachment to the planet. Thus we might think of Israel as God's clearing house for what He wishes to do in the larger scheme of things. The words spoken to Abraham are still relevant, that through His seed all the nations of the world should be blessed.

I will bless those who bless you, and I will curse him who curses you; and in you all the families of the earth shall be blessed.

- Genesis 12:3

Jesus, the ultimate Prophet, in the classic prophetic discourse of Matthew 24 & 25, refers to no other prophet of the Old Testament but Daniel, giving him a special place of honor.

The book of Daniel has but 12 chapters, half of which tell his story and his experiences in kingly courts, the other half being a series of prophetic visions.

Of all the visions, Daniel 9 is a critical piece, summarizing the whole future history of God's people Israel. It is noteworthy that the special revelation of the seventy weeks (Daniel 9:24-27), which is the subject of this chapter, is given after an intense time of prayer on the part of Daniel. He is not only engaged in serious intercession, but even confesses the sins of the nation as if they were his own.

The angel Gabriel comes to Daniel in response to that prayer with urgency, *'being caused to fly swiftly'* (Daniel 9:21), and speaks of Daniel's increased understanding as a result of the revelation being given:

Chapter 4

The Seventy Weeks of Daniel

> *O Daniel, I have now come forth to give you skill to*
> *understand.... Therefore consider the matter, and*
> *understand the vision.*
>
> - Daniel 9:22-23

There is an interesting play on the number 70 in this ninth chapter. Daniel's prayer of intercession was prompted by his reading of Jeremiah (Daniel 9:2) and through this he was reminded that God had destined 70 years of captivity for the Jews, and that those 70 years were coming to their conclusion. Is there not a meaningful parallel in the conclusion of those seventy years of captivity and displacement and judgment, and the eventual conclusion in history of Seventy Weeks of Years that will finally conclude all the captivities and dispersions and judgments that have befallen the nation?

While the first half of the book is mainly historical, it does contain the dream of Nebuchadnezzar with all of its prophetic implications, depicting as it does the major Gentile super powers yet to come, ending with the Stone without hands (a picture of Christ) shattering the earthly kingdoms and inaugurating the eternal Kingdom of God.

The history of the Jewish people would continue to be unfolded in the context of these earthly powers until the eventual Finale of God's Kingdom. These earthly kingdoms, powerful as they were, would come and go, while God's seemingly fragile people would remain, apparently indestructible, to eventually fulfil His divine purposes, not only to be recipients of God's blessing, but to bless all nations as well, as God had always intended.

Let us now turn to those four verses, Daniel 9:24-27, which contain the revelation of the seventy weeks. It is a longer text, and it is significant that the text be presented in its entirety:

Seventy weeks are determined for your people and for your holy city, to finish the transgression, to make an end of sins, to make reconciliation for iniquity, to bring in everlasting righteousness, to seal up vision and prophecy, and to anoint the Most Holy.

- Daniel 9:24

Know therefore and understand, that from the going forth of the command to restore and build Jerusalem until Messiah the Prince, there shall be seven weeks and 62 weeks; the street shall be built again, and the wall, even in troublesome times.

- Daniel 9:25

And after the 62 weeks Messiah shall be cut off, but not for Himself; and the people of the prince who is to come shall destroy the city and the sanctuary. The end of it shall be with a flood, and till the end of the war desolations are determined.

- Daniel 9:26

Then he shall confirm a covenant with many for one week; but in the middle of the week he shall bring an end to sacrifice and offering. And on the wing of abominations shall be one who makes desolate, even until the consummation, which is determined, is poured out on the desolate.

- Daniel 9:27

First of all, verse 24 speaks of 70 weeks, or literally, "seventy sevens". That these sevens could be considered as years is illustrated in a number of Scriptural precedents, including the story of Jacob and Rachel in Genesis 29:18, 20,27, and 28. Jacob was willing to fulfill Rachel's week, whereby seven years is intended in this passage.

In Leviticus 25, in the context of Sabbath regulations, verse eight says, *'the time of the seven Sabbaths of years shall be to you forty-nine years'*. If we accept this interpretation, we are dealing with a total time frame of 70 x 7 years, or 490 years of future Jewish history.

The statements in this verse speak of massive global changes, basically putting an end to sin, and ushering in an age of righteousness. These things will happen after the judgments depicted in the book of Revelation, and after the devil has been bound for a thousand years, thus allowing planet earth for once to experience the kind of peace and tranquility and prosperity for which it was created in the first place. Nothing that man has done to the planet will keep God from realizing the plan for its eventual redemption. Isaiah 45:18 declares, *'Thus says the Lord, Who created the heavens, Who is God, Who formed the earth and made it, Who did not create it in vain, Who formed it to be inhabited...'*

Note the reference to *'the holy city'* in Daniel 9:24. On the one hand, God often speaks jealously of "my land", but He is also particularly zealous for His city and for His temple. It is noteworthy that of all the great cities of the world, God has named one that shall be the center of His future government, namely Jerusalem.

Daniel 9:25 begins to break up the Seventy Weeks, or 490 years, saying that between two specified events there shall elapse 69 weeks, or 483 years. This leaves one "week" of seven years yet to come. The starting event for those first 69 weeks is given as the command to restore and build Jerusalem.

Sir Robert Anderson of the late 19th Century, in his book, The Coming Prince, calculated that from the time of Cyrus the Persian who extended the call to rebuild Jerusalem, given on March 14, 445 B.C., to Palm Sunday April 6, 32 A.D. was exactly 483 years of 360 days each (the Jewish year), or 173,880 days.

In Daniel 9:25-26, we see the picture of Messiah the Prince, and also, the Messiah cut off. Was not Palm Sunday that special day of his presentation as King, only for Him to be cut off in the week that was to follow? Even on the cross we have the awful irony of the superscription in three languages: *Jesus of Nazareth, King of the Jews.* But these were mocking words on the part of the Jewish leadership who would have their king crucified, calling on their rival Gentile powers to execute the heinous deed.

> *...the street shall be built again, and the wall, even in troublesome times.*
>
> - Daniel 9:25

Was not the rebuilding of the wall one of the most amazing stories of restoration, taking place in the midst of much opposition, as recorded in the book of Nehemiah, and completed in an unbelievable time frame of 52 days, according to Nehemiah 6:15?

Daniel 9:26 speaks of the cutting off of Messiah, which is alluded to in Isaiah 53:8: *'He was cut off from the land of the living'*. Surely if the divine life span is one of 70 years (Psalm 90) then Jesus in his early thirties was cut off in the midst of life. He was cut off, but not for Himself, the text continues. Surely this was Jesus, Who would come to save His people from their sins (Matthew 1:21). Surely this was the Lamb of God Who came to take away the sin of the world (John 1:29).

Because the world would not receive God's Prince of Life, there was another prince waiting in the wings, who would come and destroy the city (Jerusalem) and the sanctuary (Temple). This literally happened under the Roman general Titus, 70 A.D.

Jesus had uttered the poignant warning on the Day of the Triumphal Entry that if the children were not allowed to sound His praise, the stones would cry out; and ominously the stones cried out in the judgment of 70 A.D. where, as Jesus had said, not one stone would remain on the other in the destruction of the temple, (Matthew 24:2).

The history of Jerusalem throughout the past two thousand years has been one of desolation. Only in this, our day, has God restored her as His sign to the world that the end of the age is at hand. Jerusalem shall play a vital role in the end time political arena. Chapters 12 and 14 of the prophet Zechariah speak to this. She will also continue to suffer casualties until her true Prince Jesus Christ comes to her rescue at the time of Armageddon, the final battle.

Who is the *'he'* of Daniel 9:27 that confirms a covenant or treaty with *'many'* for one week? Is this the end time prince, the antichrist, posing as the benefactor to the Jewish people, condoning their sacrificial ritual, contributing to the restoration of the temple, protecting them from their enemies, perhaps in the wake of some major aggression? This has been the traditional explanation, and may be our best understanding for the time being.

The implication of the Seventy Sevens is that whereas the first 69 have been fulfilled; the countdown discontinued with the cutting off of Messiah, and there would remain that final one week to be fulfilled at the end of the age.

It is true that the book of Revelation along with other parts of Daniel speak repeatedly of a three and a half year period, speaking to events which are probably concurrent with each other. There are at least 11 such references between the two books, expressing this time frame in years or times, as three and a half; 42 months, or 1260 days. These 3 and a half year periods are generally considered to be the time of tribulation which constitute the last half of the seven year period spoken of in Daniel 9:27. The fact is that no other passage in Scripture speaks of the full seven year period at the end of the age, so a lot of burden rests on this one verse and our understanding of it.

It may be that the first 3 and a half year period is a time of false peace, even as in Hitler's time there was peace and promise for the German nation until hostilities brought destruction to Germans as well as to Jews. This period of peace might well be exemplified by the first white horse seen in Revelation, the sixth chapter.

It is significant that Jesus, speaking about Daniel's prophecy in Matthew 24, asks us to note exactly that sign which will represent the breaking of the treaty that has been made, by the *'abomination of desolation'* sacrifice in the temple.

What is the abomination of desolation? For the Jews to see a pig, an unclean animal offered as a sacrifice on the temple altar, as happened during the Maccabean period before Christ, was an expression of ultimate abomination. Should the Antichrist engage in a similar abominable act, he might well in that moment be exposing himself for who he is truly is, and cause massive reaction by the Jewish people, resulting in "desolations" on the Jews whom he now persecutes, and eventual desolation on the head of the desolator himself, according to verse 27.

In the second chapter of 2 Thessalonians, the Antichrist is called by the titles, man of sin, son of perdition, and lawless one. It says in 2 Thessalonians 2:4, that he *'opposes and exalts himself above all that is called God, so that he sits as God in the temple of God, showing himself that he is God'*. This act of abomination then, with Antichrist sitting in the temple as if he were God, results in great reaction, conflict, judgments and "desolations". There is a boomerang action in the end, a plan where evil eventually recoils upon its originator, even as in the case of Haman, who built gallows for Mordecai to be hanged, only to end up hanging there himself!

There are many doubles in God's economy. There is an Old Testament and there is a New Testament. There is a First Coming of Christ and a Second. It is interesting that on the occasion of the First Coming, Rome was in power, and there were moments of confrontation between Jesus, King of kings and the power of Rome.

One of these times was at the tomb where the body of Jesus had been laid, and where it was now guarded by a Roman watch lest his body be stolen by the disciples, and they should spread word that He had risen from the dead. When He indeed rose from the grave that glorious Easter morning, those Roman guards were smitten to the ground as dead men (Matthew 28:4). It was not to be their day!

Paul speaks of the significance of this event in Acts 17:31:

> *He has appointed a day on which He will judge the world in righteousness by the Man whom he has ordained. He has given assurance of this to all by raising Him from the dead.*

Many believe that part of the end time scenario is a revived Roman empire, typified by the ten toes of Nebuchadnezzar's image in Daniel chapter two. Antichrist is expected to come out of that context. However that may be, the same resurrected Christ will yet again face the final man of sin, causing the ultimate confrontation of good and evil, and we know Who will win!

In conclusion, there are references in Scripture to God's special dealings with Israel being laid aside for a period of time, during a time of spiritual blindness, ushering in a time of the Gentiles. Then again, the time of the Gentiles comes to an end, of which Jesus makes reference in the context of the restoration of Jerusalem in Luke 21:24:

> *Jerusalem will be trampled by Gentiles until the times of the Gentiles are fulfilled.*

Are we now in this transition time, where the Jewish clock is ready to be reactivated, thus introducing that final week, those final seven years of this prophetic writing in Daniel?

The word rapture does not appear in our English bibles, but it is used in the Latin Vulgate translation of 1 Thessalonians 4:17. However, the truth of the rapture of God's people being caught up to be with Christ at His Coming, is taught in the above passage, as well as in 1 Corinthians 15. The term used in the Thessalonians passage is *'caught up'*. The Corinthian passage in chapter 15:51-52, declares that · *'we shall not all sleep, but we shall all be changed'* while the dead are raised incorruptible.

There is little or no argument among evangelicals about the fact of the rapture. The question of timing is another matter.

My wife and I were brought up, along with so many in our generation, to believe in the so-called pre-tribulation rapture. We were taught these truths in our local Bible School, which was probably typical of many other bible schools of the day. As my wife puts it, she felt that certain theological presuppositions prompted people to read into some verses, things that the Scriptures did

Chapter 5

The Rapture Question

not necessarily say. The teaching was that of a two phased Second Coming. Jesus would come first for His saints at the Rapture; then, possibly seven years later, after the Tribulation time, He would be returning with his saints to judge the world.

Years later I was challenged through a series of events, to review this position, and in the process I reread the entire New Testament with the objective of letting it say whatever it wanted to say without trying to force it into some premeditated plan. After this exercise I became convinced that the Scriptures spoke of one Second Coming, not two; also, that the translation of the saints would take place after tribulation, not before.

Some of the pertinent Scriptures included Matthew 24, where Jesus, the ultimate Prophet, is outlining future events. He very clearly refers to the Great Tribulation in verses 21 and following. Then in verse 29, He speaks of what comes *after* the tribulation, and in verse 30 says:

> *...then the sign of the Son of man will appear in heaven...and they will see the Son of man coming on the clouds of heaven with power and great glory. And He will send His angels with a great sound of a trumpet, and they will gather together His elect from the four winds, from one end of heaven to the other.*

I would assume the "elect" to refer to Christ's people, represented by the disciples to whom He was speaking.

Another significant Scripture is found in 2 Thessalonians, chapter two. Verse one is an obvious reference to the rapture, speaking of *'our gathering together to Him'*. Verse three then says: *'Let no one deceive you by any means, for that day will not come unless the falling away comes first, and the man of sin is revealed, the son of perdition...'* The man of sin here is an obvious reference to the antichrist.

Let me share a few comments about the book of Revelation here, which is the one official prophetic book of the New Testament. The first verse of chapter 4 where John the seer is told to *'Come up hither'* has been depicted as the rapture call by some pre-tribulationists, thus allowing the church to escape all the tribulations described in the ongoing chapters of Revelation. Is this not an example of reading into Scripture something that it does not really say? I believe it is.

It has also been said that since the word "church" is not found mentioned in the book of Revelation after chapter three, that therefore the church is removed from the tribulation that follows. On the other hand, I would make the point that the whole message of Revelation was especially given to all of these churches, see chapter one, verse 4: *'John, to the seven churches which are in Asia...'* They were then also given individual messages, as recorded in chapters two and three, but the prophetic message, in its entirety, was theirs to digest and process. Would it not seem strange that this message would be given them, only to see the very carriers of this message to be immediately evacuated once the time of trouble began?

As I was reviewing the Scriptures on this topic, I asked the question: Is there anywhere in the texts dealing with this subject, even a hint at the timing of the rapture? There was a statement in 1 Corinthians 15 that caught my attention. Paul is saying in verse 51f,

*Behold, I tell you a mystery: We shall not all sleep, but we shall all be changed-in a moment, in the twinkling of an eye, **at the last trumpet**. For the trumpet will sound, and the dead will be raised incorruptible, and we shall be changed.*

So then I asked: Is there anywhere in the prophetic Scriptures, a series of trumpets, so that one could point to one, and say, this is the last. Of course, the book of Revelation has such a series. They are contained in the seventh Seal, introduced in chapter eight, and after some other interpolations, the trumpets come to their finale in chapter 11. We read in verse 15:

Then the seventh angel sounded: And there were loud voices in heaven saying, 'The kingdoms of this world have become the kingdoms of our Lord and of His Christ, and He shall reign forever and ever!'

The following verses go on to speak of what the sounding of this trumpet entails, including the rewarding of the saints. Verse 18 says:

The nations were angry, and Your wrath has come, and the time of the dead that they should be judged, and that you should reward your servants the prophets and the saints, and those who fear your name, small and great, and should destroy those who destroy the earth.

If the above passages did not answer all of my questions immediately, certainly they got my attention. Eventually, as I kept searching, my sense was that the burden of Scripture pointed to rapture later rather than sooner in terms of the end times drama.

Another question that needs to be asked is: How has God dealt with His people in times past? Did He typically rescue them out of crisis situations, or deliver them in the midst of affliction? Consider Israel in Egypt in the context of the Ten Plagues. They were not delivered out of Egypt at that point in time, but rather delivered from the plagues that were happening around them, making God's protection even more obvious and dramatic. Consider some excerpts from the Psalms.

A thousand may fall at your side, and ten thousand at your right hand; but it shall not come near you. Only with your eyes shall you look, and see the reward of the wicked.

- Psalm 91:7-8

I have done a study of texts that indicate the saints will be there to *see* judgment happening around them, while experiencing God's providential care. Psalm 23 contains the intriguing phrase, *'Thou preparest a table before me in the presence of mine enemies'*. It seems to fit in with God's way of doing things, that He demonstrates His grace and power in the midst of challenges. We need to let God deliver us in whatever way He sees best, even as in the case of Daniel's three friends. They confessed they did not know whether they would survive the fiery furnace or not; but one thing was clear, they would be true to their God, and leave the results with Him. We know the glorious end of that story; and we also know through Hebrews 11, and other passages, that many of God's faithful servants had to pay with their lives because of their courageous stand for truth.

The question has also been asked: If we in the West, who have lived so luxuriously and unhindered for so long, preach this doctrine of escaping tribulation, how will this be understood by our brothers and sisters in China, Russia, and so many countries of the world that have faced persecution, where God's people have already experienced all the tribulation one could imagine? Corrie ten Boom was one who declared that missionaries preaching this doctrine had done the believers in China a disservice, by not preparing them for the awful crises that lay ahead. Jesus made it a point to say, in John's Gospel, chapter 15, that his disciples were not to expect better treatment than had been accorded Him:

> *If they have persecuted Me, they will persecute you also.*

Paul having just survived a stoning attack in one of his missionary travels, exhorts the believers and says, *'We must through many tribulations enter the kingdom of God.'* (Acts 14:22).

There is no question that Christianity has lived with favor in the Western world ever since the time of Constantine; but the winds of change are blowing. We have entered into a climate of pluralism, where the Christian church is no longer enjoying so many of the unique benefits of the past, and where it is needing to compete on a level playing field with other ideologies for the souls of men. Interestingly, this is exactly where the early church found itself, and she was victorious in that day to make an impact for God in spite of incredible opposition and challenge.

George Eldon Ladd, in his book The Blessed Hope, makes a case for the church going through tribulation on the basis of Scripture, and supported by the records of the early church fathers. He still calls Christ's Coming the blessed hope, because the blessedness of our hope is not necessarily to escape trouble, but it is the anticipation of the Lord Himself.

It is interesting that folks like the Negro slaves in America raised the level of awareness of their faith even as their lives faced unparalleled grief and injustice and suffering. They have given us the legacy of the Negro Spirituals as a testimonial that the blessedness of our hope has nothing to do with our circumstances, but is rather lifted up when troubles increase.

Naturally, we all want to escape trouble. One of the biggest preoccupations in life is security. We seek to protect ourselves against violence, against theft, against accident, against health hazards, etc. Unfortunately, it is not our wishful thinking that determines what God has decreed about our future. The basic reality is that God will bring a sinful world to judgment, which is *'His strange act, His unusual act'* (Isaiah 28: 21). This is a necessary bottleneck of history (see chapter seven), which will then lead us into the new release of His kingdom on earth, beginning with the Millennium and beyond. Should it be God's will for His people to be part of that bottleneck (tribulation time), to be a witness of God in troublous times, and to help bring in an unprecedented harvest of souls, so be it.

Pre-tribulationists tend to confuse two biblical terms that ought not to be confused: tribulation and wrath. They will say that God has not appointed His people to wrath, and they will quote chapter and verse. We would agree that God's people are not subjected to the wrath of God, for they have already dealt with that by taking their stand under the cross, where Jesus took the judgment for all sins upon Himself. But tribulation is another matter, and we question our exemption from that.

It needs to be added that the pre-tribulation position is a relatively recent interpretation in the context of church history. George Eldon Ladd of Fuller's Seminary wrote "The Blessed Hope" in which he makes several statements to this effect.

• The pre-tribulation interpretation dates back to the early nineteenth century in England. A man by the name of J.N.Darby was particularly instrumental in teaching this view, and he visited America six times between 1859 and 1874 with this teaching, where it was warmly received.

- The view that the church would go through tribulation was the dominant view of the church fathers through the centuries. In a chapter, titled The Historic Hope of the Church, Ladd refers to ten sources verifying their position in this regard.

Another question I hear people asking is: What about imminency? Have we not always been taught the Lord could come at any time? Does not the Bible say that He will come as a thief in the night?

I believe these questions must be answered in the balance of what may seem like two opposite truths.

My sheep hear my voice, and I know them, and they follow Me. And I give them eternal life, and they shall never perish; neither shall anyone snatch them out of my hand.

- John 10:27-28

It is common for the Bible to present two views, like two sides of the same coin. One example would be found in John 10:28, which speaks of the security of the believer. Yet verse 27 brings out the human response, which is what we need to follow.

In terms of the rapture timing, the Scriptures keep saying that certain things have to happen, and only then will the end come. On the other hand, when the Lord actually does come, there will be a major problem of unawareness, of worldly preoccupations, so that people will be caught napping if they are not spiritually in tune.

Differences in interpretation of when the Lord will return should not cause breach of fellowship. I have appreciated the ministry of brothers who hold other views from those expressed in this chapter, and have ministered with such. The greatest concern is that we lift up the truth of Christ's returning, which unfortunately has been largely neglected by many in the church. But it is also important that we keep seeking the Scriptures about issues that could affect our preparedness for His return, and I believe that the Lord will continue to shed increasing light as we enter the end time zone.

It is ironic that in the time of Isaiah, one of the greatest Old Testament prophets, Jewish folk were tempted to get their futures and fortunes fixed by spurious and occult sources, rather than by the prophet of the living God in their midst. Isaiah rebukes such with the words of chapter 8:19, (Living Bible):

> *So why are you trying to find out the future by consulting witches and mediums? Don't listen to their whisperings and mutterings. Can the living find out the future from the dead? Why not ask your God? Check these witches' words against the Word of God...because I have not sent them; for they have no light or truth in them.*

Is it less ironic that in our day, with all the light of Scripture available to us, many people today go to the horoscopes, the occult, and to eastern religions for their spiritual needs?

How wonderful that God has given us His Word, and it is both a Word for the present and a Word for the

Chapter 6

A Possible Scenario of Prophetic Events

future. God has indeed spoken; He has not left us in a vacuum.

On the one hand, we need to humbly confess that there are many things even in God's prophetic word we do not understand, and perhaps some things have been purposely hidden until the time of fulfillment. On the other hand, many things are clearly described, and we need to take note of these. The intriguing balance of what we can know and what we don't know is beautifully stated in Deuteronomy 29:29:

> The secret things belong to the Lord our God, but those things which are revealed belong to us and to our children forever, that we may do all the words of this law.

I have often heard the words, "All the signs of the times requiring fulfillment before Jesus comes have already happened..." I beg to differ; I believe that some striking signs have happened and others have yet to occur. Walk with me through this chapter and test if these things are so.

I mentioned earlier, the phenomena in the early verses of Matthew 24, which have often been touted as signs, but regarding which Jesus says just the opposite: 'Don't be deceived, the end is not yet.' These kinds of things have happened throughout history. People were often tempted to think that they were omens indicating the end of the world, but time proved them wrong.

The budding of the fig tree was mentioned in chapter three. We believe this to be a reference to Israel's return to her land after two thousand years. This truly is a miracle and a sign that has never before happened. Speaking of a possible scenario of future events, this could well be our starting point. Following Jesus' reference to the fig tree in Matthew 24:32, he comments in verse 33:

So you also, when you see all these things, know that
He is near, at the very doors.

It may well be that in the context of Israel's restoration there are wars, ethnic conflicts (nation against nation), famines, pestilences and earthquakes. Note that verse 8 of Matthew 24 says, *'All these are the beginning of sorrows'*, the word sorrows referring to a woman in travail. Many Scriptures employ similar imagery, where even the earth itself convulses under the burden of sin, unrighteousness, and bloodshed, waiting for the redemption of the Son of God. Romans 8:19-22 says:

...the earnest expectation of the creation eagerly
waits for the revealing of the sons of God. For the
creation was subjected to futility, not willingly, but
because of Him who subjected it in hope; because the
creation also itself will be delivered from the bond-
age of corruption into the glorious liberty of the chil-
dren of God. For we know that the whole creation
groans and labors with birth pangs together until
now.

Another interesting Scripture is found in Matthew 19:28, Jesus speaking of the *'regeneration, when the Son of Man sits on the throne of His glory...'* This is one of only two references in the New Testament where the term regenera-

57

tion is used, and this is one of them. The other reference, Titus 3:5, speaks of personal regeneration, and Matthew 19 speaks of the regeneration of the earth when Jesus returns. God is renewing men for a renewed earth.

A second outstanding sign is the restoration of the city of Jerusalem, falling into Jewish hands on June 6, 1967. Various Christian leaders have made reference to Luke 21:24 in this connection, saying that prophecy was fulfilled that day. As Luke 21:24 states, *'they will be led captive into all nations. And Jerusalem will be trampled by the Gentiles until the time of the Gentiles are fulfilled.'* From that day forward Jerusalem was taken out of Gentile hands and restored to Jewish oversight. Nevertheless, there is an intense battle going on for the jurisdiction of this city, even as there is on ongoing debate about the land of Israel itself. The best of human mediations are proving inadequate to resolve the long standing issues affecting the opposing factions. I agree with a commentary I recently read, that the events of the Middle East are inexplicable apart from an intense spiritual battle in the heavenly realms, playing upon the peoples concerned. The devil knows that God destined a land and a people for a special purpose for His kingdom, as part of the end times finale of history, and the devil will do everything in his power to thwart God's plans.

Major geopolitical alignments have been taking place around the globe ever since World War II. The names of the nations of Africa alone read like a new slate of titles. It is interesting that in the gospels, whereas Matthew and Mark speak of the budding of the fig tree, Luke mentions not only the fig tree, but 'all the trees'. I quote from Luke 21:29: *'Look at the fig tree, and all the trees...'*

A major development in our day is the revival of Europe. It seems striking that after would-be conquerors like Napoleon and Hitler sought to unite Europe by force and failed, that there has come a moment in our times when Europe is joined together without bloodshed. What was touted at first as a union for economic benefit, is now seen as having strong political clout as well. Many believe that the feet and toes of Daniel 2, the image in the dream of Nebuchadnezzar, represent an end time variation on the Roman Empire, and this might well refer to the Europe of our day. If Europe does not answer to this end times expression of political power, the question left begging is: what does?

From our vantage point today, the suggestion of Europe would seem plausible.

Certainly Europe is flexing its political muscle as well as its economy. The common currency, the Euro has just been introduced, and movement from one country to another has been greatly expedited. It is interesting that particularly with regards to the Middle East, the voices of Europe have become increasingly assertive, and have even gone so far as to boycott Israeli goods when they deemed Israel's military actions inappropriate.

What else needs to happen before Christ descends onto the Mount of Olives, and destroys the opposing armies of Armageddon, and establishes his Kingdom in Jerusalem? Unfortunately, there is a bottleneck through which history must pass at the end of the age before the Kingdom of God appears; this bottleneck is the theme of chapter seven.

You might ask, Why must this be? Does this age of history need to end with a catastrophic "big bang"? It appears that God allows sin to become exceedingly sinful at the end of the age, so that human depravity can show itself for what it truly is. God allowed Pharaoh to rise to his full height of pride and spiritual opposition, and then God moved in to demonstrate once and for all that He alone was on the throne. It will be the same at the end of our age.

We expect a man of sin, the antichrist, to appear, who will pretend to be a world savior, but like Hitler, he will become an architect of rebellion against God and all that is good and right. Various Scriptures allude to this man; probably the most detailed passage is found in Revelation 13, where he is described simply as *'the beast'*. Daniel 9 seems to refer to him making a contract for peace for seven years with Israel, and so it may be that he will play the savior role at a time of crisis for Israel, only to break the contract and betray her later in the middle of the seven year contract period, as pointed out in chapter four.

The man of sin will show his true colors when he defiles the temple, according to 2 Thessalonians 2:4, and sits in the temple as if he were God.

...[the man of sin] opposes and exalts himself above all that is called God, so that he sits as God in the temple of God, showing himself that he is God.

- 2 Thessalonians 2:4

Thus, there must be a temple. I expect a temple will be built, and it may well be that antichrist himself will build it as a 'favor' to the Jews. If he did, this would not be without historic precedent-consider King Herod building the third temple, which became the temple of Jesus' day.

The matter of defiling the temple, the 'abomination of desolation' was one of the specific signs Jesus pointed to in answering the disciples' questions. It was the first time that he said *'when you see...'* in answer to the question of signs.

...when you see the abomination of desolation, spoken of by Daniel the prophet, standing in the holy place...

- Matthew 24:15

The question of building a temple on or near the site of the present Mosque of Omar is one of the most volatile issues affecting not only the Middle East, but even larger world interests. For Islam, this is their third holiest shrine. With all the conflict and animosity between Arabs and Jews, it is hard to imagine what it would take to allow for a temple to be built. Yet it must happen. When and How are intriguing questions.

There is an intriguing aside that I see in Scripture that seems to have been largely overlooked-namely, strong statements to the effect that Jesus Himself will build the eventual millennial temple. Probably the strongest words to this effect are found in Zechariah 6:12-13:

> *Behold, the Man whose name is the Branch!...He shall build the temple of the Lord; Yes, He shall build the temple of the Lord. He shall bear the glory...*

I am also reminded of Jesus' words at the cleansing of the temple in John 2:19, *'Destroy this temple, and in three days I will raise it up.'* Surely it is not beyond the realm of possibilities that the Creator of the Universe who made the world in six days, could recreate a Temple in three days if He so chooses! The Temple referred to here is the same as Ezekiel describes in such great detail toward the end of his prophecy.

Part of the bottleneck of the end times are the battles and wars, largely against Israel. There is a Gog and Magog war, which may well include Russia and associates. Ezekiel chapters 38-39 speak to this issue. Secondly, there is a Far East army of 200,000,000 mentioned in Revelation 9:16, which might well involve China and other forces in that region. At no time in history do we know of a nation mustering an army of 200 million, but China has already boasted that figure for her armed forces. Finally, there is a gathering of nations from all over the world at Armageddon against God Himself. It is at this point that Christ descends, and destroys the opposition. Psalm Two is a poetic description of this event, and Revelation 19:11-21 is probably the more definitive reference to this landmark battle of battles.

Babylon is a big word in Scripture, representing human opposition to God's purposes. Babylon will be destroyed by God as part of the end time scenario. But are we sure what Babylon means? Is it a restored city in the present country of Iraq, as some affirm? Or is it some other city that represents earthly glory and spiritual indifference? Is it western civilization? Is it the United States?

At the end of 1 Peter, chapter 5, verse 13, Peter sends greetings from "Babylon". This is likely a pseudonym for Rome, and if so, would indicate that the name expresses a spirit as much as a place. This kind of thing happens with other names in Scripture as well.

Babylon's demise is described in two chapters in Revelation, chapters 17-18, as well as two other earlier passages in the same book. It would seem to have economic clout as well as moral and spiritual significance. Babylon is also dealt with in the later chapters of Jeremiah and in several passages of Isaiah.

I expect that when the time of fulfillment comes, we will understand who Babylon is, and say with Peter, '*This is that...*'. I recently read a book detailing the story of the massacre at Tiananmen Square in Beijing, China, in June of 1989 where some ten thousand students were killed by Chinese authorities. The book, by Gordon Thomas, speaks especially to the indifference of the western powers to this tragedy, putting their business interests above *'the souls of men'*. This expression, the souls of men, is found in the context of Babylon's destruction in Revelation 18, and seems a poignant reference to what happened on that fateful day. Revelation 18:12-13, speaks of all the kinds of merchandise the trades people will be mourning over, and after a list of some 27 items, mentions, *'the souls of men'*.

Coming back to the words of Jesus in Matthew 24, there are two messages that Jesus repeated over and over. These were: don't be deceived, for in the last days there will be a lot of deception. Secondly, those will be times of stress and persecution, so be ready for that. It is so easy to be preoccupied with the excitement of signs, and not heed the messages of concern that Christ repeated for our benefit.

When Jesus spoke of the parables of the kingdom in Matthew 13, he said *'the harvest is the end of the age'* (Matthew 13:39). The parable of the wheat and the tares begins in verse 24. They represent a double harvest, a harvest of evil, and a harvest of good. Note that according to verse 30, the tares are gathered up first.

When Peter spoke on the day of Pentecost, he quoted Joel. In the context of cataclysmic end time events, he said, *'Whosoever shall call upon the Name of the Lord shall be saved.'* (Acts 2:21). God will have the last word in the harvest of men. When men see the world around them collapsing, many will call on His name. See also Psalm 46. When Israel has discovered their true Messiah, and become the world's greatest missionary force, many will be garnered into the kingdom.

God has all kinds of resources at his disposal to bring in the harvest. There is a strong Scriptural reference to Elijah coming at the end of the age to prepare the way for Messiah to return. I am well aware that John the Baptist was the "Elijah" preparing for the first coming. I believe, however, that there is an Elijah yet to come. It is interesting that this has been a Jewish tradition over the centuries, and at the occasion of their Passover celebrations, a special chair is reserved for Elijah, and during the ceremony a child is sent to the door to see if he has come! One of the clearest references to an end time Elijah is found in the last paragraphs of the Old Testament:

> *Behold, I send you Elijah the prophet before the coming of the great and dreadful day of the Lord. And he will turn the hearts of the fathers to the children, and the hearts of the children to their fathers, lest I come and strike the earth with a curse.*
>
> - Malachi 4:5-6

Is this Elijah one of the two prophets described in Revelation 11:3? It might well be that these are Moses and Elijah, the same two prophets that spoke with Jesus on the Mount of Transfiguration, Matthew 17:3.

In summary, speaking of possible scenarios, we need to affirm our limited understanding of many details. We may know more of specific events than we know of when they will happen, or the sequence in which they happen. But that should not keep us from being reminded of the information we have been given. The events which have we referred to in this chapter could be listed as follows:

1. Israel restored to her land,
2. Jerusalem restored to Jewish jurisdiction,
3. Europe emerging as a new economic and political entity,
4. The destruction of Babylon,
5. The rise of Antichrist,
6. The building of an interim temple,
7. The harvests of evil and good,
8. The ministry of Elijah and Moses,
9. Three end time battles, ending with Armageddon,
10. Jesus returning to the Mount of Olives and Jerusalem and establishing His kingdom.

We should not terminate this chapter without making some reference to the great events following the days of judgment and battle. Once Jesus has defeated the enemy forces at Armageddon, there follows a thousand year millennial period, where peace reigns on the earth, and men's swords have been turned into ploughshares. The devil is bound for these thousand years, only to be released for one final battle at the end, after which he is cast into the lake of fire.

Revelation 20 describes the Great White Throne judgment, where all the dead appear before God, and those whose names are not found in the Book of Life face eternal judgment.

The final two chapters of Revelation then describe the new heaven and the new earth, which will be the eternal home of all those who have loved the Lord throughout the centuries of time.

Paul speaks of times of stress in his letter to Timothy, *'But know this, that in the last days perilous times (or, times of stress) will come...'* and he goes on to characterize these times:

> *...men will be lovers of themselves, lovers of money, boasters, proud, blasphemers, disobedient to parents, unthankful, unholy, unloving, unforgiving, slanderers, without self-control, brutal, despisers of good, traitors, headstrong, haughty, lovers of pleasure rather than lovers of God.*
>
> - 2 Timothy 3:1-4

Much of what he says in these verses reflects the kinds of conflict and violence we read about in our daily newspapers. I am reminded of Dr. A. H. Unruh, my professor in Bible College, speaking of the text in Matthew 24:12, which reads, *'Because lawlessness will abound, the love of many will grow cold.'* Dr. Unruh referred to this love as speaking of natural human relationships as in the family and the marriage. It would seem as if the glue which had kept

Chapter 7

Days of Stress, Bottleneck of History

society together would no longer be holding.

Jesus uses the word tribulation, and speaks of its stress levels as unprecedented.

Matthew 24: 21 states: *'For then there will be great tribulation, such as has not been since the beginning of the world until this time, no nor ever shall be.'*

Mark adds some slight variations in his text and I will add two verses here:

> For in those days there will be tribulation, such as has not been from the beginning of creation which God created until this time, nor ever shall be. And unless the Lord had shortened those days, no flesh would be saved; but for the elect's, whom he chose, He shortened the days.
>
> - Mark 13:19-20

Not only do both writers attest to a coming tribulation that will be unprecedented, but they speak to the survival of God's people only due to God's divine intervention.

There seems to be indeed a bottleneck of history, through which we must pass, from which we emerge into a new era of God's "seventh day" of millennial peace. Perhaps we could even compare this time of stress to the experience of the caterpillar, who suffers through the strictures of the cocoon before he emerges as the beautiful butterfly he was destined to become.

The book of Revelation, the one designated prophetic book of the New Testament, depicts in some detail, this kind of bottleneck at the end of the age. At the same time, it tells the story of the triumph of the kingdom of Christ, and the triumph of God's people. It has become very meaningful to me, that this book of Revelation, containing the graphic descriptions of the coming tribulation in chapters six through 19, begins with a revelation of Christ Himself. Chapter One features this disclosure of Christ in all of His glory, and when John sees Him, he falls down as a dead man. It is noteworthy that nowhere in all of the difficult images in the rest of the book does John fall down as being overwhelmed by them. Is this not a great illustration of the fact that he who would be overwhelmed by the risen Christ need never be overwhelmed by times of trouble? What a great lesson of keeping things in perspective; of observing a holy balance in difficult times!

The book of Revelation is a fitting closure of all that has been spoken (prophetically) in all the previous prophetic utterances of Scripture. Not only do we meet the awe inspiring Christ at the beginning of the book, before the tides of judgment; but by the end of the book we are brought to the actual scenarios of victory for Christ and His people.

But the question may well be asked, "Why should history have to end in a series of judgments like this?" Ever since the fall of man, man's pride has propelled him to extend his ego to the limits. Lucifer, who wanted to exalt himself to be like God (Isaiah 14:12-15) has set this negative model for the human race, which has affected and infected all human kind. Later in history, man built a tower of Babel

(Genesis 11) to reach to the heavens, to challenge the God of the heavens. The nation that God then especially called to be his people, Israel, became notorious for substituting other gods for the one true God who had chosen them. It was because of this sin that they were eventually taken into captivity.

Mankind in general tends to live his life without acknowledging the God who created Him. In recent centuries so called scientists have promulgated the evolutionary theory of tracing human origins to some slimy green algae instead of giving honor to God our Maker. On the other hand, man remains incurably religious, and so he accepts new versions of eastern religion and calls it the New Age. He vainly declares he has discovered God within himself!

Can we understand that at some point in time God has had enough of all this nonsense, this human pride, self-sufficiency, and vain conceit?

The bubble of human vanity is not yet full blown, however, but will come to its culmination through the man of sin, the antichrist. He is the number 666, mentioned in Revelation 13:18 that can never attain to the perfection of God's perfect number, seven, but he will appeal to the end time world as a savior, probably making his debut at a time of world crisis.

Jesus speaks of the ripening of harvest, both of evil and of good, in Matthew 13, and in antichrist we have the personification of the ripening of evil. Somehow God in his wisdom allows evil to do its worst before He steps in and pronounces judgment.

There appears to be a trinity of evil imitating the divine Trinity, and so in antichrist you have a human being imitating the true Christ. He will be the visible expression of the invisible satan who possesses and inspires him. The Scriptures even speak of him having a deadly wound that was healed, imitating Christ's resurrection from the dead. Revelation 13:3 says:

I saw one of his heads as if it had been mortally wounded, and his deadly wound was healed. And all the world marveled and followed the beast.

There is also a false prophet aiding and abetting the antichrist, even as the Holy Spirit is always lifting up Christ. This is discussed in Revelation 13:11-15.

A bottleneck is generally a small fraction of the bottle itself. So the bottleneck of history is limited. A three and a half period of time is mentioned in the book of Revelation some five times, and several more times in the book of Daniel. All these references may well apply to the same period of time, the time of tribulation.

It is generally believed that antichrist may well come onto the scene as Israel's deliverer, and make a covenant for seven years (Daniel 9). Then he will break the covenant he has made at its mid point, and that leaves three and a half years of persecution and tribulation. It is interesting that at no other point in the prophetic Scriptures are we given such a strong time frame, repeated over and over. Could it be that those who will be subjected to these times will find incredible comfort in the fact that God is keeping his stopwatch in hand, and will call for the time according to His good judgment. Surely, *'my times are in your hands.'* (Psalm 31:15)

Hitler was a kind of forerunner of antichrist, obviously obsessed by evil aspirations and passions, but he did not get to win the world as he had hoped. He was seen as a savior to his people, and did many good things for his country, but it was in the end that his true nature became obvious to all.

Antichrist will have world wide powers. He will control the world economy, allowing no one to buy or sell but those who have 'the mark'. He will be a man of bloodshed, seeking to eliminate those who refuse to worship him as god.

Alongside antichrist's antics, the God of heaven will be stirring the heavens, shaking the earth, disturbing the regular patterns of weather, sun, moon and stars, to let the citizens of the planet know Who is in charge of the universe. The Lamb who was authorized to open the seven seals (Revelation 5) is in the process of opening them, and the contents of the chapters six through 19 of that signal book spill out throughout the earth as the finale of the harvest of evil.

All this God allows to transpire before Christ triumphantly returns to take His rightful place as God's appointed Regent, and to reign from Jerusalem. (Isaiah 2, Micah 4).

I had made a list of some of the global issues affecting us today, and I will share that list here. Let me preface that by saying that we have indeed become a global village compared to any other time in history, as witnessed by our incredible mobility, transportation, and communication technology. This tendency towards globalism might in itself be a prophetic signal, since the Scriptures speak of the world of the end times as a united entity.

Here is my list. I have put it in alphabetical order so as not to presume which has priority of importance:

- Climate and weather changes
- Diseases and plagues, such as AIDS, of which 6000 people die daily in Africa alone
- Drugs, and drug trafficking, and drug related violence
- Earthquakes, and other acts of God, like volcanoes, tornadoes, and hurricanes
- Economic concerns, nationally and internationally
- Famine, food shortages
- International dynamics, tensions between peoples, nations, ethnic conflicts
- Israel's role in world peace; status of Jerusalem involving three world religions
- Mid-east tensions
- Moral collapse of traditional and family values in the western world
- Nuclear, chemical and bacteriological weapons build up
- Pollution of atmosphere, water supplies
- Population densities
- Space, threats of meteorological collisions, U.F.Os
- Spiritual indifference
- Terrorism, violence

I have kept clippings and statistics on many of the above issues for years, and you might well have done the same. It is probably correct to say that while many of these factors have been present in past generations, they have not come together en masse as they do today to threaten our future.

We cannot speak of a future bottleneck of history without making reference to the nuclear age in which we live. My dear Uncle Abe Friesen, who just passed away a year ago at the ripe old age of 93, had given me a book many years ago by Wilbur M. Smith, professor at Fuller's Seminary in California. The book was written in 1948, and was entitled, *This Atomic Age and the Word of God*. Dr. Smith spoke of the new age of physics into which we had entered as a fulfillment of Scripture. He also spoke strongly to the effect that through these developments we might well have ushered in the final days of the present age.

The atomic bomb was used by the United States on two Japanese cities in August of 1945, and probably helped to bring an end to World War II. It is remarkable, that no other nuclear device has been used against human kind since, and it is now 57 years since Hiroshima and Nagasaki. Does this mean that the powers that be have kept each other at bay through some kind of balance of terror? Does it mean that we have just been lucky till now, though we know there have been some 'close calls'?

Unfortunately, there has never been a weapon developed in the history of the human race that was not eventually used. On the other hand, the good news is that God will not allow nuclear war to destroy this planet. It would appear that nuclear weaponry might well play a part in the scenes of Revelation and other prophetic passages, but man will not be allowed to destroy himself. Of late, the phrase in Revelation 11:18, has become increasingly reassuring, that Christ will come to *'destroy those who destroy the earth.'* The God who oversaw creation will also oversee the dissolution of things, and preserve that which He chooses to preserve.

There is much more to be said about the present day alignment of nations, and the geopolitical realities of the day, and where they might be taking us in the future. Look for more on this in chapter nine: The King and the Kingdom.

How easily we can fall into a doomsday mind-set. It is difficult sometimes for God's people and even God's prophets to maintain a proper balance. How was Jeremiah to behave as he stood at the very brink of the judgment that was to befall his beloved people, his city and their temple? Was he to party and dance with them, when he knew that the enemy was lurking at the doors? Yet even for Jeremiah, caught as he was, at the end of an era, there were beautiful glimpses into that glorious future that God had prepared for His people.

We too struggle for a holy balance. We are not doomsday prophets. We see a world in rebellion against its Creator, and this calls for redress. Judgment must come, but there is always hope for God's people in the end. We must be incurable optimists, because our faith and trust is rooted in the very God of hope (Romans 15:13).

As we may be approaching times of challenge, let me draw your attention to a parable Jesus gave us in Matthew 13, namely, the Sower and the Seed. Referring to the seed that fell among the thorns, verse 22, he says:

> *Now he that received seed among the thorns is he who hears the Word, and the cares of this world and the deceitfulness of riches choke the Word, and he becomes unfruitful.*

It strikes me that there are two opposite responses mentioned here, that apply also to the above Word of prophecy. On the one hand, we can be filled with anxiety (cares) instead of prayers, overwhelmed with fear for that which is happening. On the other hand we can carry on business as usual, without paying attention to warning signs, which is exactly what Jesus said was happening in Noah's day, and what would happen again in the days before His return (Matthew 24:37-39).

May God again grant us balance, that we fall into neither of these ditches, but remain on the moral and spiritual high ground of focused expectation and preoccupation with His Coming Glory and His Kingdom.

Bottlenecks are always limited time frames; beyond them lies the fulfillment of God's eternal purposes.

Jesus did not leave us unprepared for hard times. He said that His followers should expect the same treatment accorded Him.

Remember the word that I said to you, 'A servant is not greater than his master.' If they persecuted Me, they will also persecute you. If they kept My word, they will keep yours also.

- John 15:20

In Mark 10:29-30 Jesus declares:

Assuredly I say to you, there is no one who has left house or brothers or sisters or father or mother or wife or children or lands, for My sake and the gospel's, who shall not receive a hundred-fold now in this time-houses and brothers and sisters and mothers and children and lands, with persecutions-and in the age to come, eternal life.

We know what happened to Jesus. There were those who didn't like the message and they killed the messenger. It has been said that the greatest resistance to the ministry of Jesus were the religious leaders of the day. In the end, in a strange collusion of forces, the religious authorities combine with the secular powers against their common enemy, our Lord.

When Jesus pronounced his indictment against the Jewish leaders, the scribes and Pharisees in Matthew 23, He indicated that theirs had been a history of resisting God's messengers through the centuries.

> *Therefore indeed, I sent you prophets, wise men and scribes: some of them you will kill and crucify...that on you may come all the righteous blood shed on the earth, from the blood of righteous Abel to the blood of Zechariah...whom you murdered between the temple and the altar.*
>
> - Matthew 23:34-35

So we are reminded in these statements that the reality of persecution has not changed over the years, and we cannot .expect better treatment in the future, despite the trappings of civilization that we like to boast about.

The apostles knew the reality of suffering for their faith: they experienced it themselves, and they wrote about it to the churches of their jurisdiction.

The Apostle Peter addressed the first of his two letters to the suffering church of his day. *'Now, for a little while'* he says, *'you have been grieved by various trials, that the genuineness of your faith, being much more precious than gold that perishes, though it is tested by fire, may be found to praise, honor, and glory at the revelation of Jesus Christ.'* (See 1 Peter 1:6-7).

The great Apostle Paul had been Saul the persecutor. At the time of his dramatic conversion he was told what a signal witness he would be, and *'how many things he must suffer for My name's sake'*, (See Acts 9:15-16). In the Greek language, by the way, the words for witness and martyr are the same. The implication is that a true witness for Christ can expect to pay the ultimate price. In Acts 14:22 the apostle Paul is instructing fellow believers, *'We must through many tribulations enter the kingdom of God.'* He is saying this in Antioch in the context of just having been stoned, and presumed dead by some of the participants. The lengthy eleventh chapter of 2 Corinthians is one extended series of incidents in Paul's life of suffering for Christ in the course of his ministry.

Writing to Timothy, his junior pastor friend, he further makes this definitive statement: *'Yes, and all who desire to live godly in Christ Jesus will suffer persecution. But evil men and imposters will grow worse and worse, deceiving and being deceived.'* (2 Timothy 3:12). Paul is writing these words in the last letter we have, as he is languishing in a Roman prison, anticipating his soon "departure".

Of the eleven apostles, we understand that all became martyrs for their faith with the exception of John, who was banished to the island of Patmos, where he received the glorious revelation of end time events and the Second Coming of Christ. You can find some further details of the martyrdom of the apostles in the first pages of Foxe's Book of Martyrs.

A point of theology: there are those who quote the Scriptures that say God's people are not subjected to God's wrath. This is clearly stated in 1 Thessalonians 4:9 and elsewhere. It is important however, to distinguish between satan's wrath and God's wrath. Perhaps the story of Israel in Egypt at the time of the Ten Plagues is a helpful illustration. Israel had been subject to Egypt's wrath. But when it came time for God's judgment, Israel was protected, plague by plague. This kind of distinction must also be taken into account when we look at the book of Revelation and other prophetic Scriptures. God has not promised to take us out of trouble, but to keep us through it, and He may choose to do this by divine protection *in the fiery furnace* or by removing us.

I wish to make the point that not only did Jesus and the apostles make statements about persecution being an ongoing reality for the people of God; but that both Jesus and the apostles point specifically to these things happening in the last days. We are often tempted to emphasize what we would like to hear and see, and may miss some vital things the Word is saying. In Matthew 24, for instance, Jesus practically tones down the signs we so often enlarge on, and says, the end is *not yet*. However, he goes on to say there will be two major realities characterizing these times. These two realities are deception and *persecution*. He mentions this over and over so we don't miss it.

The book of Revelation written to seven churches is a reminder to those churches of persecution being a fact of life in the last days. It describes several scenes of martyrdom, including chapter 6:9-11 (fifth seal), and chapter 7:9-17 (the great multitude).

Foxe's Book of Martyrs is a reminder to us of persecutions happening through the centuries. Paul Marshall's book, Their Blood Cries Out, is a very recent book describing what is happening in our times. We are told that more people have died because of their faith in Christ in the last century, than in all the centuries past. It is amazing that in the day of the global village, that we in the west know so little of the suffering of brothers and sisters in Christ in other countries around the world. It has been said that not only are we ignorant, but that we would rather not know lest it make us uncomfortable!

The ministry of *Open Doors*, with Brother Andrew, publishes a World Watch Persecution Index ranking the top 20 countries of the world where the persecution of Christians is most severe. I have studied the latest copy, published in 1995, which includes Saudi Arabia, Iran, Sudan, Comoro Islands, China, North Korea, Qatar, Egypt, Oman, Morocco, Libya, Maldives, Yemen, Somalia, Mauritania, Vietnam, Afghanistan, Algeria, Turkey, and Pakistan. The very least we can do is to pray for our brothers and sisters going through persecution, and encourage our churches to do the same in corporate intercession.

For some time now I have been in receipt of a monthly magazine, *The Voice of the Martyrs*, wholly given to covering this topic. Each issue tells graphic stories of individuals who have been caught up in persecution situations, and these become specific targets of intercession.

I want to add Billy Graham's voice to our list of references here. In his book about Billy Graham, *The Evangelist*, Lewis A. Drummond devotes an entire chapter to 'Billy Graham and Suffering'. He alludes to some of the early church martyrs, seeing their suffering in the light of eternity. Ignasius, who was martyred for Christ in 110 A.D. is said to have cried out, "Nearer the sword, then nearer to God. In company with wild beasts, in company with God." There is a story told of how Graham's own ministry was under attack, and it was his son Franklin who reminded him that this was a spiritual battle, instigated by the father of lies who is forever resisting the purposes of God.

We in the west have not seen much of violent persecution for our faith, and often glibly think it can't happen here. Some of us have parents and grandparents who came from other countries where freedoms were suddenly lost. My parents came from Russia, where Mennonites had enjoyed over 100 years of freedom and great liberties. Suddenly all that changed as the nation was catapulted into revolution, accompanied with anarchy and social upheaval.

We ought to consider the possibility that our world of freedom could change also. Are we prepared to pay a price for our faith, even our lives? It is true even now in our country that Christianity is often the target of mockery and contempt. In our politically correct society it is considered very narrow minded to question the life style of gays, but churches, pastors and Christians are ready subjects of ridicule by the media.

Are there voices speaking out today, warning us about the possibility of persecution? Billy Graham again, in a message entitled 'Joy in Tribulation' states: "Nowhere does the Bible teach that Christians are to be exempt from the tribulations and disasters that come upon the world. It does teach that the Christian can face tribulation, crisis, calamity and personal suffering with a supernatural power that is not available to the person outside of Christ."

Corrie ten Boom, a holocaust survivor, says she was given a divine mandate to tell the Christians in the United States to prepare for persecution. She said, "We are in training for the tribulation...There are some among us teaching there will be no tribulation, that the Christians will be able to escape all this. These are false teachers Jesus was warning us to expect in the latter days...In China the Christians were told, 'Don't worry, before the tribulation comes, you will be raptured.' Then came a terrible persecution. Millions of Christians were tortured to death. Later I heard a bishop from China say sadly, 'We have failed. We should have made the people strong for persecution rather than telling them Jesus would come first.'"

Corrie was not speaking as an arm chair theologian, but as one who had been through the tribulation of a concentration camp, and at 80 years of age was prepared to face with joy and the power of the Holy Spirit whatever lay before her.

We should be encouraged by someone like Corrie and others who have actually tasted persecution. Did not the negro spirituals emerge as a tribute of faith in the midst of oppression? Looking at a page of my Bible in Revelation 6 and 7, I am impressed with the cry of the martyrs, not for their pain but for their brothers. The voices crying out in anguish are the lost unsaved souls who call out to the rocks and the mountains to fall on them because they are seeking to escape the wrath of God.

I have several copies of a very special event entitled, *The Forty Martyrs of Sebaste*, telling of an elite legion of the Roman army of the 4th century, who were faced with a choice between allegiance to Caesar or Christ, and the 40 who chose to die for their faith were sent to the center of a frozen lake. There was a heated bathhouse by the shore for any who would recant. They spent those last hours singing. One of their songs was, *Forty good soldiers for Christ*, until one returned and the group continued with *39 soldiers for Christ*. Then the jailor became a believer and joined those singing martyrs and the theme again was 40 soldiers. They died that day as a tribute to their faith, praising God to the last.

The promises of God were given for times of need. Are there promises not yet cashed in? The Psalms are full of God's promises for his people, for times of trouble. Take Psalm 91 as an example:

> *He who dwells in the secret place of the Most High shall abide under the shadow of the Almighty...Surely He shall deliver you from the snare*

of the fowler and from the perilous pestilence...A thousand shall fall at your side, and ten thousand at your right hand; but it shall not come near you. Only with your eyes shall you look, and see the reward of the wicked.

Obviously not all believers will be martyred, for the Scripture speaks of *'those who remain,'* (1 Thessalonians 4:17). Many demonstrations of God's protection, provision, and direction will undoubtedly occur. And for those who are called upon to pay the ultimate price, may they see themselves in a holy alliance with Stephen that first martyr whom Jesus seems to have given a special welcome into His heaven. This is the only instance where Jesus is described as standing rather than sitting at the right hand of the Father. Does this speak of the Lord's special sensitivity towards those who have given their lives in martyrdom?

It was Jim Elliott, who as a young missionary to Ecuador, died as a martyr with four other men, in 1956. He had earlier penned the words: "He is no fool who gives what he cannot keep to gain what he cannot lose."

The Lord's Prayer teaches us to pray, *Thy Kingdom Come.* Not only does this attest to the reality of a future Kingdom of God, but there is also the implication that the prayers of God's people will make a difference towards its realization.

There will come a day when the great pronouncement of Revelation will be fulfilled, as the seventh Trumpet is sounded:

> *The kingdoms of this world have become the kingdoms of our Lord and of His Christ, and He shall reign forever and ever.*
>
> - Revelation 11:15.

Those of us who have heard Handel's great Oratorio, the Messiah, or even had the opportunity to sing it, will forever echo the words of that glorious refrain, sung by powerful voices and accompanied by majestic musical instruments. How much greater yet will be the reality when this transition of all powers on earth will be properly vouchsafed into the hands of Him Who is the rightful heir to the throne!

Chapter 9

The King and The Kingdom

Before we consider that eventual Kingdom, I want to comment briefly about the *'kingdoms of this world'* as they appear today. Something has already been said about the realignment of nations following World War II. Israel was restored to nationhood in 1948, and Europe has taken on a new unity.

On September 11, 2001, the United States was attacked by four hi-jacked airplanes, two of which brought down the twin World Trade Towers in New York City. Since that day, there has been a new awareness that there are people 'out there' who hate the west, and who hate America, and who are committed to its demise. President George W. Bush has gone so far as to name an 'axis of evil' mentioning the countries of Iraq, Iran, and North Korea. It seems that for political reasons, the U.S. seems cautious about which countries it has not yet named!

For the past several years, I have had the opportunity, largely through the Internet, to tune in to a series of news sources who care nothing about political correctness, and who share the facts as they see them. One of these sources has been Joseph Farah, and his web site, World Net Daily (WorldNetDaily.com). Another has been Jeff R. Nyquist (JRNyquist.com), who also has his own web site on the Internet at this time.

There is ample evidence, according to these sources, and many others, that the U.S. role in world hegemony is being seriously challenged by the most powerful nations in the eastern world, Russia and China. These countries are not only amassing weaponry for a coming conflict, they are also aiding and abetting other nations in the process. Major defectors from both Russia and China have offered evidence to this effect to western authorities, but it seems we are living in such a climate of appeasement and negotiation, that it is hard for us to imagine who our enemies are, or what they might be up to.

The question has been asked as to the place of the United States in Bible prophecy. There seems to be limited material here that one would want to be dogmatic about. The very fact that the prophetic Scripture does not include America may beg the question as to whether she will still be playing a major role in the last days scenario. If God needs to judge Babylon in the closing days of the age, there may also be a spirit of Babylon on our continent that He needs to address.

Many prophetic words and warnings have been spoken about major crises coming to the U.S., beginning with General Washington, who became the first President. George Washington had a major angelic visitation one day during the Revolutionary War, where he was told of three great catastrophes that were yet to befall America. The first was the then current War of Independence; the second pointed to the Civil War of the mid 1800's; the third was to be the most severe, where America would be attacked from several directions, and though she would survive, she might well lose her place of prestige among the nations.

The question has also been asked, Where is Canada in the context of the east versus west struggle? In many ways, we share the moral corruption of our neighbor to the south. However, we are also a separate entity, and it may be that we will play a role of mercy if America should be attacked, even as this happened in part on the occasion of September 11, where unexpected planeloads of people landed in Canadian airports, and were given a fine taste of Canadian hospitality.

So, if one knew nothing of Bible prophecy, and listened only to 'secular prophets' who don't care about political correctness and yet see barbarians approaching at the gates, we have reason to be concerned about major changes that may be in the offing for a spoiled western world.

However, knowing Bible prophecy, we know that God will allow all of these nations to move only as He wills, and that in the end His Hegemony alone will be established in the earth!

Jesus made his entry onto our planet, when Rome was the symbol of power. While He did not challenge that political power directly, He began His public ministry with the declaration that *'the kingdom of God is at hand'* (Matthew 4:17). John the Baptist did the same (see Matthew 3:2). It is striking that at a time in the Jewish economy where Jews were not in charge of their own affairs politically, where they were obviously under the mastery of Rome, and after having passed through several centuries of subjugation under various nations, that both John and Jesus would announce the imminence of the Kingdom of God!

Would these announcements arouse questions in the minds of reactionaries that this might be the time to shake off the yoke of the Roman overlords? Would Jesus need to clarify that for the time being, the kingdom would be invisible? Luke 17: 20-21 states: *'The Kingdom of God does not come with observation...indeed, the Kingdom of God is within you.'* Even after the resurrection the disciples are still trying to sort things out, and ask, *'Lord, will you at this time restore the kingdom to Israel?'* (see Acts 1:6). And He answers, *'It is not for you to know times or seasons which the Father has put in His own authority.'* Then in verse eight He goes on to talk about the Spirit enabling them to witness, which would bring men into the invisible Kingdom.

There is a Kingdom invisible and a Kingdom visible. How do we define the Kingdom of God as such? The Kingdom of God represents the total rule of God. All of creation, from eternity to eternity is His dominion. Yet within that creation, He made beings that were given the freedom to willingly submit to His lordship or rebel against it. Unfortunately there were angels that rebelled, and that led to the human race that fell. While planet earth is enduring the coup of the usurper satan, there emerges an invisible form of God's Kingdom which awaits the planet earth's liberation through God's rightful Regent, King Jesus.

The King is none other than Jesus, God's Son. Of Him, the Father says, in Psalm Two, *'Yet I have set my King on My holy hill of Zion.'* Indeed that whole Psalm is one of the most graphic descriptions of the end time battle of rebel nations, and God's installation of His Son.

Let me quote a few more lines:

> *Ask of Me, and I will give You the nations for Your inheritance...You shall break them with a rod of iron; You shall dash them in pieces like a potter's vessel. Now therefore be wise, O kings; be instructed, you judges of the earth...*

Unfortunately, the eventual proclamations of Christ's Kingship do not come without judgment upon those who refuse to bow to Him voluntarily. How sad that we need to deal with all the events of Revelation six through 11, and again 12 through 19, before men allow God to rule. Thus follows the wrath of God, His 'unusual act' about which all of the prophets have written. (See Isaiah 28:21).

Paul expresses the truths of Christ's kingship in 1 Timothy 1:17, *'Now to the King eternal, immortal, invisible, to God who alone is wise, be honor and glory forever and ever. Amen.'* And again in chapter 6:14- 16, *'our Lord Jesus Christ...who is the blessed and only Potentate, the King of kings and Lord of lords, who alone has immortality, dwelling in unapproachable light...to whom be honor and everlasting power. Amen.'*

The life of Jesus seems such a contrast to royalty, as Jesus did not even enjoy the common amenities of life. He never married. He had no home address. He owned no property.

Yet kingship is intertwined throughout the life of Jesus. The angel tells Mary in Luke 1:32-33, *'the Lord God will give Him the throne of His father David. And He will reign over the house of Jacob forever, and of His kingdom there will be no end.'* Isaiah the prophet had said in Isaiah 9:6-7:

> *Unto us a Child is born...and the government will be upon His shoulder, and His name will be called...Prince of Peace. Of the increase of his government and peace there will be no end, upon the throne of David and over His kingdom...*

As already mentioned, the kingdom was the opening note of Jesus' message, and He continued to talk about the kingdom. The church is mentioned only twice in all the gospels, but the kingdom many times.

One might ask at this point: What is the relation between the church and the Kingdom of God? The Kingdom is the eternal rule of God over all of His creation, voluntary or otherwise. The church is the unique body of willing responders to the grace of God, who in this present age form the invisible aspect of the kingdom, yet to come in all its full expression.

After the feeding of the 5000 mentioned in all the gospels, there were those who wanted to make Jesus king right then and there, but again Jesus prevents this-the timing was premature.

On Palm Sunday, the day of the triumphal entry into Jerusalem, Jesus permitted the believers and the children to declare his kingship in Luke 19:38, *'Blessed is the King who comes in the name of the Lord.'*

Again on the Cross, His kingship is proclaimed by Pilate and the superscription over the cross in three languages: "Jesus of Nazareth, King of the Jews." He might have had his ulterior motives for doing so, but nevertheless the proclamation was made. When he was challenged about it, he stood his ground for once, and said, What I have written, I have written!

These proclamations of kingship, in the context of rejection and crucifixion, leave the question begging, What kind of kingdom is this?

The way of the cross, God's plan for forgiveness, was to pave the way for an invisible kingdom of men who would receive divine rule in their lives not because it was forced upon them but because they chose to receive it.

Thus a King embraces a cross, to allow for a temporary invisible kingdom, to emerge in God's own time as the visible expression of God's rule.

We too, as God's people, awaiting the eventual kingdom for which all of creation groans (see Romans 8) face a cross of our own. By definition, let the cross represent those unpleasant elements of life we assume because we have chosen to follow Christ. There is also a bottleneck at the end of the age, already referred to in chapter seven, where the believer may face suffering, even death, because of his devotion to His Savior. Jesus said this should not surprise us. If, for Christ, the way to the Kingdom led through the cross, we must be prepared for those kind of possibilities.

Yet we too await kingship. Peter describes even our present status as *'royal priesthood'* in 1 Peter 2:9. Revelation 1:6 declares that Christ *'has made us kings and priests to His God and Father...'* Paul says in 2 Timothy 2:12, *'If we endure, we shall also **reign** with Him.'* Jesus Himself spoke on various occasions of the rewards given his servants, and that they would be given jurisdiction over territories and cities (See Luke 19). How gracious that God not only forgives us our sins through Jesus; that He not only receives us into His family; but that He also bestows on us the blessings of partnership with Him for now and the eternity to come, of which we have only such limited awareness! 1 Corinthians 2:9 says:

> *Eye has not seen, nor ear heard, nor have entered into the heart of man, the things which God has prepared for those who love Him.*

Amid all the uncertainties of our personal futures, and of the world around us, one thing is absolutely certain: Jesus is King, and He is coming back to reign, and we will reign with Him. There is a beautiful summary passage in 1 Corinthians that wraps up the eternal arrangements of lordship and kingship and submission even in the context of the divine trinity.

> *Then comes the end, when He delivers the kingdom to God the Father, when He puts an end to all rule and all authority and power. For He must reign till He has put all enemies under His feet...But when He says all things are put under Him, it is evident that He who put all things under Him is excepted. Now when all things are made subject to Him, then the*

*Son Himself will also be subject to Him who put all
things under Him, that God may be all in all.*

- 1 Corinthians 15:24-28

May these aspirations lead us to pray with ever greater fervency the last prayer of the Bible: *'Even so, come, Lord Jesus!'* (See Revelation 22:20). There is a Scripture as mentioned earlier that hints at our hastening the day of the Lord through our lifestyle and prayers. 2 Peter 3:12-13 speak of us *'looking for and hastening the coming of the day of God...Nevertheless we, according to His promise, look for new heavens and a new earth in which righteousness dwells.'*

The words of this chapter title are taken from 2 Peter 3:10-11, and are spoken in the context of world judgment:

Chapter 10

What Kind of People Ought We To Be?

> *The day of the Lord will come as a thief in the night, in which the heavens will pass away with a great noise, and the elements will melt with fervent heat; both the earth and the works that are in it will be burned up. Therefore, since all these things will be dissolved, what manner of persons ought you to be in holy conduct and godliness...*

The thrust of prophetic Scripture is always to challenge our personal life styles and our holiness. Prophecy is not to satisfy the whims of our curiosity; it has been given to prepare God's people for the challenges of the end of the age. It is also there to instruct and inform God's people of things they will need to know to properly conduct their affairs in those last days.

As I have shared this message in various places and settings, I have arranged the answer to the above question in a series of W's...namely, God's people should be Word-centered, Wise, Willing, Warm, Waiting, Working, Watching, Warning, Winning, Witnessing, and Worshipping. Thus we have a chapter with these 11 sub headings.

Word-centered

We have already indicated in chapter One, that any balanced view of Scripture will include an interest in prophecy, since more than one quarter of Scripture is prophetic. From the same book of 2 Peter as our title above, we are told, *'we...have the prophetic word made more sure, which you do well to heed as a light that shines in a dark place, until the day dawns, and the morning star rises in your hearts...'*

I refer again to John Wimber, the father of the Vineyard Movement, saying, "The only word God has pledged himself to honor is His own." That is a meaningful statement in the context of many words that have been spoken in the name of the prophetic. Certainly it is right that all human utterances are examined in the light of Scripture, and only as they align themselves with the Divine Word do they merit consideration.

Given the preponderance of prophetic truth in Scripture, it is worth reminding ourselves that so much of that material bears on the great finale of history, which we might well be in the process of seeing fulfilled before our eyes. 1 Corinthians 10:11 states that the Old Testament instruction was *'written for our admonition, on whom the ends of the ages have come.'*

How can we claim to be Word-centered in the pulpit if there are virtually no messages reminding us of the coming of the Lord? How can we claim to be Word-centered if we don't at least read the prophetic text? The book of Revelation is the only place in the Bible that offers specific blessing to those who read it.

Wise

Daniel 12:3 says, in the context of the end times, *'those who are wise shall shine like the brightness of the firmament.'* Both knowledge and wisdom become significant in the context of the last days, but there is a big difference between the two. Knowledge is mentioned in verse four, saying, *'knowledge shall increase.'* If we are looking for signs of the times, certainly the increase of knowledge has become phenomenal.

When on tour in Israel in 1983, Marvin Forseth, put it this way: in roughly 4000 years of human history, knowledge had doubled only once. From 1800-1900 it doubled again in only 100 years. By 1969 it was doubling every 10 years; by 1973, every five; and by 1978 every two and a half! Thus we are dealing with an exponential curve of information that is continuing to explode. Having access to the computer and to the internet, there is such an endless parade of information as to be mind boggling.

Certainly the traffic of information is making the world a smaller place, and is giving way to the concept of a global village, which might well eventually play into the hands of anti-christ who will seek to control the planet.

There is nothing wrong with being informed; we cannot imagine Daniel as Prime Minster in his day, as putting a premium on ignorance. But the difference between knowledge and wisdom is the application of the information we have to the achievement of meaningful purposes, or godly ends.

Jesus made the meaningful statement that *'wisdom is justified by her children'*. I think of Noah as an example. Noah's contemporaries could have laughed him off as the greatest fool, building an ark on dry land; but his kids knew how smart their father was, having survived the flood on the ship Noah built. Many times God's wisdom is just the opposite of human wisdom, and for this reason we have to be willing to put up with some misunderstandings and even opposition; and be prepared to wait till all the evidence is in.

The many references to wisdom characterizing God's people at the end of the age leads me to believe that there will be a special dispensation of divine understanding to help guide believers in the understanding of the Word, interpreting current events, guidance in terms of actions that may be required of them for their own protection, and for the proclamation of the gospel in special days of spiritual harvest.

Willing

Psalm 110 is one of the great Messianic Psalms, and verse 3 says, *'Your people will be willing in the day of your power.'* Can you imagine anything sadder than God's people not being ready to move when God is moving? We have sought to show through the previous chapters that God is at work in special ways in our day, fulfilling the prophetic word, so these should be times for maximum spiritual alert.

I decry the fact that in our own denomination there was a strong expectation of the Lord's Coming some 40 years ago, and now all these years later, we have become strangely silent. Are we truly prepared for what God is speaking to our generation? One of my College professors, J.A.Toews, once made the comment that those who have the most difficult time discerning what is happening to their moment of history are the people who live at that moment of time. We are too close to the trees to see the forest. That is why we need seers, and that is why we need to listen to their vision.

Our problem is not inactivity! It may be we have too much activity, even spiritual activity. The well known story of Mary and Martha may be apropos, reminding us that only as we take the time to listen to the Lord will our activities be pleasing and rewarding. I heard a prophetic word given a while ago which stated, "Do no uncommanded work." May God keep us from being so busy with so many programs that we miss the 'good part' Jesus spoke to Martha about.

Warm

The word should really be very warm, or *hot*, based on Revelation 3:15-16. Christ speaks out against the lukewarm condition of the church of Laodicea, and says, *'I could wish you were cold or hot.'*

In my counseling I have often asked the question, 'Was there ever a time when your love for Jesus Christ was greater than it is right now?' If there is even a moment's hesitation in the response, spiritual homework may be indicated.

It is in the first of the seven letters, the one written to Ephesus, that the Lord registers the indictment: *'Nevertheless, I have this against you, that you have left your first love.'* Similar to the above comments under 'Willing', these believers were known for their works and their labor, but not for their love. How sad!

In Paul's last recorded letter, 2 Timothy, he challenges us not only regarding our love to the Lord, but that we love His appearing. Rephrasing the verse, he says:

> *...the Lord, the righteous Judge, will give me the crown of righteousness on that Day, and not to me only, but also to all who have loved His appearing.*

> - 2 Timothy 6:8

Waiting

In 1 Thessalonians 1:9-10, Paul, speaking to these new believers, says they turned to God (faith) from idols (repentance) to serve the living and true God, and *to wait for his son from heaven.*

Jesus used the picture of the bride waiting for the groom, already referred to above. Can you imagine a groom separated by overseas duties, longing to be reunited with his beloved? Would it make a difference to him how she conducted herself? For her to be waiting would consist of more than punching a time clock. She would be involved in any possible communication; she would be preoccupied with her personal enhancement and readiness. The worst thing the bride could do would be to start flirting with other men since her lover was out of sight.

All these comparisons give us pause to meditate on what it means for the church to be waiting for the divine Bridegroom.

There is a chorus that expresses the true call of the waiting bride:

Even so, Lord Jesus, come,

Our hearts do yearn for Thee!

Come and take thy people home!

Even so, Lord Jesus, come!

Working

1 Thessalonians also speaks of God's people serving. (See 1 Thessalonians 1:9). As the saying goes, we are *'saved to serve'.*

Jesus spoke of believers as servants, in the context of the last days, awaiting their due rewards at the end of the day. The parable of the talents in Matthew 25, speaks of servants who are entrusted with solemn responsibilities in the Lord's temporary absence, poised to give account in the day of His return. The message of the book of Revelation was entrusted to His servant John (Revelation 1:1) to pass on to the churches, and through them to the believers through the centuries till their Lord returned. By the way, what a service it was that John rendered, banished on the isle of Patmos without the conveniences of a modern study or word processor, to nevertheless faithfully record the message God gave Him, to comfort and equip the church for her task.

The context of Matthew 25 also indicates that effective work takes place as we use the gifts God has given us. People have become newly aware of the whole area of spiritual gifts in the last decade or two. Knowing your gift and using your gift will bring pleasure to you as well as those you serve. Working outside of your gift will do the opposite, and may prove hazardous to your health.

Billy Graham has wisely questioned the place of retirement for God's people, and has modeled an ongoing service into his later years. Certainly there may be a slowing down of activity as our bodies age; but one could well deplore the many good years that have been wasted on the part of people who took early retirement and limited the impact they might have had building God's kingdom.

It is intriguing to think that there is no such thing as unemployment in the kingdom of God. One is left only to choose out of so many options, where to spend ones time and energies. My guess is that as our world proceeds towards more troubled times, the opportunities for service will only increase.

Watching

Jesus used this word a lot when speaking of His return. I have counted 10 references. A similar admonition is found in Ephesians 5:15-16: *'See then that you walk circumspectly, not as fools, but as wise, redeeming the time, because the days are evil.'*

Note the word *circumspectly.* Breaking it down, "spectly" reminds us of spectacles, which enable us to see; while "circum" reminds us of a word like circumference, or something round. The message is that we walk with our eyes wide open, taking in all that is happening around us, especially in anticipation of the Lord's Return.

As I think of the oft used phrase, Watch and pray, I think of a double awareness, watching for what is happening in the world around us; and praying to God for his direction in light of what we are seeing.

In a sense that was what Daniel was doing. He saw the visions, and then he looked to God for what to do with this information.

Today by Television we can literally be watching, and not just hearing, the news of the day. By the way, we can also make choices as to what news we listen to, and seek to find objective information in the midst of a lot of biased material.

Then we bring the information we have to our Heavenly Father, and He helps us to interpret it.

Throughout this entire study the underlying presupposition has been that while we do not set dates, we ought to look out for signs and seasons, and we have two instances of Jesus chiding his hearers because they were ignorant of their times while claiming to be good weather forecasters.

Warning

Colossians 1:28 says, *'Him we preach, warning every man...'*

We live in a culture of growing moral laxity. It is interesting that Jesus would describe the last generation as *'adulterous and sinful'*, (see Mark 8:38).

When the Roman Empire fell, it was not because of the barbarians from without as much as because of the moral laxity within. Someone once quipped that it is dangerous to have the air conditioning on (a symbol of creature comfort) because your windows will be closed and you won't hear the enemy coming.

When Jesus compared the time of His coming to the days of Noah, he implied that people would stubbornly persist in 'business as usual' to the day of their doom. See Matthew 24:36-44. They specifically did not have time for the seer Noah, and his dire warnings. May God help us to do better on this last round of judgment facing the planet.

As I see it, we are being served with a double warning at this hour in history. Not only do we have the Word of God warning us about all the ways we can be caught unawares;

but we also have the so called secular prophets, like the people who set the Doomsday Clock, warning us about dire dangers down the road. September 11, 2001 was a great wake up call for the west, but in many ways it seems we have turned back to our soft life styles.

Speaking to the soft underbelly of our culture, Robert Bork, in his book, *Slouching Towards Gomorrah*, comments, "American popular culture is in a free fall, with the bottom not yet in sight. This is what the liberal view of human nature has brought us to...There is an eager and growing market for depravity, and profitable industries devoted to supplying it."

Winning

Daniel 12:3, speaks of the Wise people also *winning* souls. This speaks to the great harvest at the end of the age, which Jesus mentions in Matthew 13:39, where He says, *'The harvest is the end of the age.'* When Peter quotes Joel on the Day of Pentecost, and says, Whoever shall call on the name of the Lord shall be saved, he is saying this in the context of a world falling apart, and men crying out to God for salvation. Probably there will be many a Bible that has collected dust over the years, that will quickly be pulled off the shelves, in order to hear a word from God. I expect that for many, it may take their world to fall apart before they call on the Lord. But God will be ready to save those who call on Him out of a pure heart. How exciting to be God's people for a time like this, and to be available as spiritual midwives for all that will yet enter the kingdom. (See Acts 2:19-21).

Witnessing

Winning and witnessing are related, but there is also a difference. According to 1 Corinthians 11:26, we *'proclaim the Lord's death till He comes'* every time we take Communion. Here is spiritual 'body language' at work.

By going to church, by being part of a believing community, by saying grace before our meals at a restaurant, we communicate that God is present in our lives.

There may come a time when there will be a price on our heads for this kind of spiritual identification, but even our death will be part of the proclamation, as has been the case with so many martyrs of the past. Again, it is instructive to consider that the same word in Greek is used for both witness and martyr, the implication being that martyrdom might well be the price that witnessing for Christ could cost us.

Worshipping

Revelation chapter five describes a crescendo of worship of our Lord, on the part of the redeemed, of innumerable angels, and finally, of all creation. (See Revelation 5:8-14).

It is interesting and instructive that throughout the book of Revelation, with all of its judgments and horrors, there may be wailing on the part of godless rebels, but you will find none of this on the part of the saints. They continue in the stance of worship, even if they should walk through martyrdom into the bliss of their Lord's presence.

The saints at the end of the chapters of tribulation and judgment, are still worshipping (see Revelation 19).

We should also be a worshipping people. We worship God for who He is. And if the world seems to become unstable and insecure at times, we know that its very insecurity will bring into new relief the Security of the One who holds the world in His hands. It is in the context of a world shaking, that we are admonished to *'be still, and know that I am God'* (Psalm 46:10).

May God help us to worship well down here, as we prepare to join one day in that choir of innumerable hosts, to proclaim forever, the praises of our God.

Blessing and honor and glory and power be to Him who sits on the throne, and to the Lamb, forever and ever.

- Revelation 5:13

109

-

In the past number of years, I have adopted a new method for my personal Bible Study. I called it Word Studies. Any question that called for further Bible research I would pursue for a given period of time, and this would invariably end up with one or more pages of written material, detailing references and commentary.

Word Studies with Prophetic Themes

Through the course of time I might come back to themes already dealt with, and I would then go back to the original material and add new insights to it.

I find that in writing down these devotional thoughts, I remain more focussed, and more alert, in contrast to merely thinking these things, or even speaking them.

To date, I have accumulated some 257 such studies, and in reviewing them now, there are 93 that relate to prophetic themes, which constitutes 36%, just over one third. If you remember, this figure relates to our earlier comments about the prophetic content of Scripture. My special interest in this field might account for the extra percentage points!

I have included the titles of these 93 themes in this appendix. Following the list, I have provided a sample outline of study #34.

These themes are indicative of the many prophetic treasures hidden in the Scriptures, and suggestive of much more one might explore, relating to questions of your interest and research and giftedness.

The themes given below are arranged alphabetically:

1. Antichrist, designations of
2. "Appearance" of Christ
3. Babylon
4. "Blesseds" of Revelation
5. Blessed is He that cometh in the Name of the Lord
6. Boomerang
7. "Business as usual" syndrome in the end times
8. Church versus Kingdom
9. "Come out of her, my people"
10. Consumption & divine judgment
11. Crescendo of conflict
12. Daniel, a type of the end time believer
13. David & the kingdom
14. David as future king
15. Day of the Lord
16. Day of trouble (Psalms)
17. Decimation of planet earth
18. Desire for the Lord's Return

19. Destroying the enemy, as Christ's action
20. Eagerly awaiting Christ
21. Earth conditions, topography, shaking, Isaiah 24
22. Earth filled with His glory
23. Earthquakes in the last days
24. Elijah of the end times
25. "End" in Scripture
26. Enemies under His feet
27. Events before Christ's Coming
28. Faith in the last times
29. Fig, vine, and olive trees
30. Finale with a flourish?
31. "Fire" in Scripture
32. "Generational" texts
33. "Holding Fast"
34. Hosts, Lord of
35. Hour of destiny
36. Impact of Christ's Coming
37. Israel, banner to the nations
38. Jerusalem in Scripture
39. Jerusalem, judgments, and promises
40. Jerusalem & Zion, in the Psalms
41. Judgments, the
42. Judgments, the fate of the ungodly
43. Kingship of Jesus in the gospels
44. Knowledge phenomenon
45. Knowledge and maranatha
46. Last day, in the gospels
47. Last days, and Jesus' First Coming
48. Millennial inhabitants
49. Mountains, hills, and valleys
50. "New", all things

51. North factor, with regards to Israel
52. Numbers, Psalm 90
53. Participation of the saints in judgment
54. Perilous times
55. Planet changes
56. Prayers (Scriptural) for the Second Coming
57. Promises in the midst of judgment
58. Prophetic messages, Psalms
59. Prophetic messages, Proverbs
60. Prophetic nuggets, the gospels
61. Protection promises
62. Rapture
63. "Remain", those who
64. Responses to end time challenges
65. Rest for the people of God
66. Return of Christ & evangelism
67. Return of Christ (Key words)
68. Revelator, God as
69. Satan's fall
70. Secrets, God's revealing of
71. "See" saints seeing God's judgment on the ungodly
72. Shaking power of God
73. "Shortening" the time of trouble
74. Signs and wonders
75. Signs of His Coming, 54 references
76. Signs of His Coming, Matthew 24
77. Sovereignty of God in judgment
78. "Strange acts" of God
79. Stress issues
80. "Suddenness" of the end
81. Temple passages
82. Temple, rebuilt by Christ

83. "Times" of tribulation
84. Topographical changes coming
85. Tribulation & ameliorating factors
86. Tribulation, our response to
87. Tribulation to Millennium, the transition
88. Understanding of latter days
89. U.S. in Bible prophecy
90. Vengeance of God
91. "Where?" question answered by Jesus in Matthew, Luke
92. Winds of judgment
93. Wrath of God

Word Study #34

Let us look more closely at one study, # 34, regarding The Lord of Hosts.

I was helped in this study by the comments of the late Dr. James McKeever, who lived in Oregon, conducted end time seminars around the country, and published a paper, entitled, End Times News Digest.

He made the striking comment that whereas we make much of names of God that are used only occasionally in the Bible, the name, the Lord of Hosts appears 262 times, and it is seldom referred to. Have we missed something significant by overlooking this name of God?

Literally, you might translate, Lord of hosts, as Lord of the armies, and as we think of a building up of opposing forces of good and evil in the latter days, this name gains special significance.

Several Scriptural images come to mind. One is the story of Elisha and his servant, where the latter saw the opposing armies of Syria, according to 2 Kings 6, and was terrified. Then Elisha, the seer of God, asked that God would open the eyes of his servant, and when he did, *'behold the mountain was full of horses and chariots of fire all around Elisha.'* (See 2 Kings 6:17). The servant then understood that *'those who are with us are more than those who are with them.'* (See 2 Kings 6:16).

Jesus, in the hour of his arrest, when his disciples were trying to protect him in their panic, declared, *'do you think that I cannot now pray to my Father, and He will provide me with more than twelve legions of angels.'* One Roman legion being 6000 men, this would constitute a heavenly army of 72,000 angels strong.

The term Lord of hosts becomes very prominent in the last two books of the Old Testament, appearing 46 times in the 14 chapters of Zechariah, and 24 times in the four chapters of Malachi. It is fitting that as these prophets spoke powerfully to end time events, the title of Lord of the armies would be a reminder that God would marshal the necessary forces to win the battle.

In the New Testament, the name appears as Lord of Sabaoth, and is found in Romans 9:29, and in James 5:4. The first of these verses is given in the context of Israel's restoration and of end time judgment. The reference in James is also given in the context of last days, see verse 3, where he speaks of social injustice, which the Lord will come to address.

I trust these comments may whet your appetite to further research the treasures and promises God has given us in His book.

Arthur I. Brown, *I will come again.*
Fundamental Truth Publishers, 1947.

Billy Graham, *Approaching Hoof-beats.*
Grason, 1983.

George Eldon Ladd, *The Blessed Hope.*
Eerdmans Publishing Company, 1956.

H.A. Baker, *Through Tribulation.*
Calvary Books.

Joan Peters, *From Time Immemorial.*
Harper & Row, 1984.

John Foxe, *Foxe's Annals of Martyrs.*
Inspirational Promotions.

John Wesley White, *Thinking the Unthinkable.*
Creation House, 1992.

J.R. Church, *Hidden Prophecies in the Psalms.*
Prophecy Publications, 1986.

Bibliography

J.R. Nyquist, *Origins of the Fourth World War.*
Black Forest Press, 1999.

Lewis A. Drummond, *The Evangelist.*
Word Publishing, 2001.

Paul Marshall, *Their Blood Cries Out.*
Word Publishing, 1997.

Rick Joyner, *The Harvest.*
Whitaker House, 1989.

Sir Robert Anderson, *The Coming Prince.*
17th Edition, Kregel Publications, 1969.

Wilbur M. Smith, *This Atomic Age and the Word of God.*
W. A. Wilde Company, 1948.

Yossef Bodanski, *Terror!.*
S.P.I. Books, 1994.